THE HEGEMONY OF PSYCHOPATHY

Fig. 1. Hieronymus Bosch, Ship of Fools (1490–1500)

The Hegemony of Psychopathy

Lajos Brons

Brainstorm Books
Santa Barbara, California

brainstorm books

First published in 2017 by Brainstorm Books
A division of punctum books, Earth, Milky Way
www.punctumbooks.com

ISBN-13: 978-1-947447-16-5 (print)
ISBN-13: 978-1-947447-17-2 (ePDF)

LCCN: 2017952337
Library of Congress Cataloging Data is available from the Library of Congress

Book design: Kyra Curry, Kristen McCants, & Jessica Morales
Cover design: Athena Tan
Cover image: Chad Person, "Kraken," 2012

Contents

Figures, Tables, & Boxes

For James.

Preface

Some people— such as Johan Norberg, Steven Pinker, and Hans Rosling— believe that the world is a much nicer place than it used to be and continues to get better and better.[1] Such optimistic claims are supported by a rather selective use of data and indicators of progress, however. Sure, some things have gotten better. Music, for example, although I accept the possibility that not everyone shares my enthusiasm for the proliferation of extreme and experimental genres of underground music of the last decades. And the personal computer I'm using to type these words is a lot more convenient than the mechanical typewriter I used as a child. Indeed, we have more and nicer stuff, but many of us are forced to work longer hours, while real wages have declined almost everywhere. Inequality within and between countries is on the rise. Job satisfaction has been destroyed by excessive bureaucracy and a culture of distrust. Depression and other mental disorders have become the number one health problem. Electronic and camera surveillance is becoming ever more pervasive. Welfare programs are cut back and coupled to increasingly repressive and demeaning measures. Nothing is safe from markets and marketing. Universities and hospitals have become factories. Racism and other kinds of intolerance never disappeared and even seem to be on the rise again. Politics have devolved into a circus controlled by the super-rich. And catastrophic climate change is looming. The world is not becoming a

---

1   Steven Pinker, *The Better Angels of Our Nature: Why Violence Has Declined* (New York: Viking, 2011). Johan Norberg, *Progress: Ten Reasons to Look Forward to the Future* (London: Oneworld, 2016). Hans Rosling is best known from a series of interesting TED Talks available on YouTube.

better place; by any standard that matters, it's getting worse. Optimism is ideologically motivated self-deception.

As a child of the 1970s, I was raised on a diet of optimistic belief in progress. The world would move towards social justice and a reduction of human suffering. The future would offer greater equality between social classes, genders, ethnic groups, and peoples. Rather naively, I experienced the 1980s as a mere temporary setback— soon the world would get back on track. It took a few decades of further destruction before I finally lost my optimism to disillusionment and anger. In her latest book, Martha Nussbaum makes the silly and somewhat offensive claim that anger involves a desire to see the wrongdoer suffer.[2] If she would be right, then a mother who is angered by her child would want that child to suffer, but while virtually all parents are angry at their children on many occasions, very few would want their children to suffer. And in case of the anger that permeates this book, Nussbaum's claim could not be further from the truth: it is the persistence of massive suffering that made me angry in the first place, and that anger is related to a strong desire for *less* suffering, not more. It is that desire that motivates this book.

Most of (the first draft of) this essay was written in the Fall of 2015, but some parts have been lifted— albeit in significantly altered form— from earlier work. Some sentences about "othering" in the first chapter come from "Othering, an Analysis."[3] In the second chapter, Box 2 (on power/authority) as well as a few other sentences come from "Anarchism as Metaphilosophy."[4] Most of the section "Education for Compliance" in the same chapter and some other sentences and paragraphs in that chapter are lifted from an unpublished talk given in 2013, "Truth, Rhetoric, and Critical Thinking."[5] And there are a few sentences in the last section of the fourth chapter that also can be found in "Facing Death from a Safe Distance:

2   Martha Nussbaum, *Anger and Forgiveness: Resentment, Generosity, Justice* (New York: Oxford University Press, 2016).

3   Lajos Brons, "Othering, an Analysis," *Transcience: A Journal of Global Studies* 6.1 (2015): 69–90.

4   Brons, "Anarchism as Metaphilosophy," *The Science of Mind* 53 (2015): 139–58.

5   The full text of this talk is available at my website: www.lajosbrons.net.

Saṃvega and Moral Psychology."[6] The epilogue, on the other hand, is newer— it was added in July 2016.

I want to express my deep gratitude to everyone who took the effort to read an earlier version of this essay and comment on it. Many of the comments I received were very helpful in improving it. Because I didn't write this essay just for an "academic" audience, I was especially pleased with the many thoughtful comments I received from "non-academics" (i.e., people who do not work in science, broadly understood). One recurring comment surprised me, however, and is worth mentioning here. Some readers appeared to have the idea that a reference to some author implies broad agreement with that author. To avoid misunderstanding, I want to emphasize here that this is not the case. For example, Robert Nozick's short paper on the Holocaust plays an important role in the first chapter (and returns in the last),[7] but this by no means implies that I share his views on social and political philosophy (for which he is far more famous). The same applies to various other authors mentioned in this essay: references are to particular texts or even to particular ideas or quotes in those texts, never to whole oeuvres.

In addition to these readers of earlier drafts, there are a few other people who I would like to thank: my students, for continuously forcing me to rethink my arguments and explanations; Takashi Iida, whose support enables my position on the academic fringe and thus also made it possible for me to write this essay (but who has not read a word of it yet); Ka Ketelmug for Figure 1; and Eileen Joy and everyone else at punctum books for publishing this "spontaneous act of scholarly combustion."[8]

Most of all, I want to thank my wife Tomoko for regularly reminding me that philosophy is useless (and for allowing me to be

---

6   Brons, "Facing Death from a Safe Distance: *Saṃvega* and Moral Psychology," *Journal of Buddhist Ethics* 23 (2016): 83–128.

7   Robert Nozick, "The Holocaust," in *The Examined Life: Philosophical Meditations* (New York: Simon and Schuster, 1989), 236–42.

8   "Spontaneous acts of scholarly combustion" is a slogan on punctum books' website. It also describes very well how I think of this little book and was one of my reasons for choosing punctum to publish it.

part of her life), and our daughter Nagi for being a source of joy in an increasingly dystopian world.

Tokyo, September 2016.

1
The Holocaust

The Holocaust has received surprisingly little attention from social and political philosophers. This is surprising because the scale and extent of the atrocities involved in the Holocaust should be impossible to ignore. If we humans can do *that,* then that makes a difference— or *should* make a difference— for our beliefs about the ideal society, for example. At the very least, we should want to organize society to avoid any recurrence.

Among the very few philosophical texts that explicitly deal with the Holocaust, three stand out as especially important— at least, in my opinion. These three are Hannah Arendt's *Eichmann in Jerusalem,* Norman Geras's *The Contract of Mutual Indifference,* and Robert Nozick's "The Holocaust".[1]

The last— at a mere 7 pages— is by far the shortest of the three, but by no means the least important. Nozick argues that after the Holocaust, "mankind has fallen" and "humanity has lost its claim to continue".[2] Of course, he doesn't deny or even play down the many other horrendous atrocities committed by men, but he maintains that the scale and extent of the Holocaust is such that it "alone would have been enough", and that "the Holocaust *sealed* the situation and made it patently clear."[3] Nozick imagines alien observers, visitors from another galaxy, looking at human history:

1 Hannah Arendt, *Eichmann in Jerusalem: A Report on the Banality of Evil* (New York: Viking, 1963). Norman Geras, *The Contract of Mutual Indifference: Political Philosophy After the Holocaust* (London: Verso, 1998). Robert Nozick, "The Holocaust," in *The Examined Life: Philosophical Meditations* (New York: Simon and Schuster, 1989), 236–42.
2 Nozick, "The Holocaust," 238.
3 Nozick, "The Holocaust," 238.

> It would not seem unfitting to them, I think, if that story came to an end, if the species they see with that history ended, destroying itself in nuclear warfare or otherwise failing to be able to continue. These observers would see the *individual* tragedies involved, but they would not see . . . any further tragedy in the ending of the species. That species, the one that has committed *that,* has lost its worthy status.[4]

Nozick goes on to ask himself whether there is anything we can do to "redeem ourselves." He suggests that perhaps,

> we need to change our own nature, transforming ourselves into beings who are unhappy and who suffer when others do, or at least into beings who suffer when we inflict suffering on others or cause them to suffer, or when we stand by and allow the infliction of suffering.[5]

The English noun "compassion" comes from Latin "*com-patī*" (through Old French), which literally means "to suffer with." Hence, etymologically, to have compassion for someone is to suffer with that someone, to share their suffering. This is the kind of compassion that Nozick points at in the above quote. A compassionate being— in this sense— is a being that suffers when others do, and therefore, if Nozick's call for "redemption" makes sense, we should be(come) compassionate beings.

Compassion should not be confused with pity, although the two are somewhat similar. Pitying someone or feeling sorry *for* someone is not the same as suffering *with* someone. Pity is inherently hierarchical— even patronizing, perhaps— while compassion is not. Compassion is an aspect or variant of *empathy,* which has become a prominent research theme in social and moral psychology as well as in ethics and the philosophy of mind. For example, the social psychologist Daniel Batson mentions "compassion" as an alternative denotation of what he calls "empathic concern,"[6] an other-oriented

4 Nozick, "The Holocaust," 238–39.
5 Nozick, "The Holocaust," 240.
6 C. Daniel Batson, "The Things Called Empathy: Eight Related but Distinct

emotion in agreement with the perceived welfare of someone in need.[7] Within the burgeoning research on empathy, "empathy" itself is not a univocal concept, however. In addition to his own notion of empathic concern, Batson distinguishes seven others.[8] Table 1 summarizes them.[9]

As Batson points out, the proliferation of concepts of "empathy" is partially due to the fact that the concept is brought in to explain two very different things: knowing what another person is thinking or feeling, and responding with care to the suffering of another person. Different mental capacities figure in these explanations, and consequently, the eight concepts of empathy in Table 1 are not just different concepts, but describe different (albeit related) capacities as well. Perhaps, rather than as concepts of empathy, they are better understood as facets or varieties of empathy.

The eight varieties of empathy play different explanatory roles, but also differ in other respects such as the degree to which they are controlled or automatic and their self / other orientation. For example, perspective taking and simulation are both controlled processes while motor mimicry and sympathy are more or less automatic. Perspective taking and simulation differ from each other in their orientation: the former is other-oriented, while the latter is self-oriented. Empathic concern and empathic distress differ in the same way: the former is other-oriented, while the latter is self-oriented.

Furthermore, many of these varieties of empathy are more or less independent abilities, and therefore, having an ability or deficiency with regards to one (or more) of these kinds of empathy doesn't necessarily imply having abilities or deficiencies with regards to the others. Some people are very good at simulation, for example, but are incapable of perspective taking (or even of understanding the difference between the two). People on the autism spectrum tend to be less proficient in some of the lower-numbered kinds of empathy,

Phenomena," in *The Social Neuroscience of Empathy,* ed. Jean Decety and William John Ickes (Cambridge, MA: MIT Press, 2009), 3–15.

7   Batson, *The Altruism Question: Toward a Social-Psychological Answer* (Hillsdale, NJ: Erlbaum, 1991). Batson, *Altruism in Humans* (New York: Oxford University Press, 2011).

8   Batson, "The Things Called Empathy."

9   Neither the terminology nor the descriptions in Table 1 are completely identical to Batson's.

Table 1: Eight Concepts of Empathy

	Concept of Empathy	Short Description
1	cognitive empathy	knowing the other's mental state (i.e., what someone else is thinking or feeling).
2	motor mimicry	mimicking the other's facial expression, posture, and/or motor action.
3	sympathy (emotional contagion)	coming to feel as the other (i.e., matching emotions).
4	projection	projecting oneself in the other's situation.
5	perspective taking	imagining what/how the other is thinking/feeling.
6	simulation	imagining what/how one would think/feel in the other's situation.
7	empathic distress	feeling distress at witnessing the other's suffering.
8	empathic concern (compassion)	feeling for the other who is suffering.

but often have no deficiencies with regards to empathic concern (although this is different for people with "full-fledged" autism). For psychopaths, narcissists, or people with an anti-social personality disorder, on the other hand, a deficiency in empathic concern (and distress) can go hand in hand with "normal" capacity for some or most of the other varieties of empathy.

While the kind of empathy that matters for Nozick's redemption is just the eighth, empathic concern, many of the varieties of empathy distinguished by Batson relate to the Holocaust in a different way. Norman Geras argues that post-Holocaust society is built on a foundation of "mutual indifference,"[10] that is, a widespread deficiency in empathic concern (and distress), perspective taking, and simulation (although he doesn't use these terms), but the Holocaust itself was made possible by selectively taking these deficiencies to their climax. The opposite of compassion is psychopathy, but the antipode of empathy in general is "othering."

The list of atrocities committed by men since the end of the Holocaust is long and depressing. For example, the Yugoslav Wars

10 Geras, *The Contract of Mutual Indifference*.

of the 1990s are less than two decades in our past, and continue to shape the region. The viciousness with which former friends and neighbors attacked each other calls for explanations and instilled in many a need to make sense of what happened. Reflecting on the war, Slavenka Drakulić wrote:

> I understand now that nothing but "otherness" killed Jews, and it began with naming them, by reducing them to the other. Then everything became possible. Even the worst atrocities like concentration camps or the slaughtering of civilians in Croatia or Bosnia.[11]

Othering is a form of dehumanization. It is the reduction of the other from other human being to mere (faceless) thing. More technically, othering is the construction and identification of the self or in-group and the other or out-group in mutual, unequal opposition by attributing relative inferiority and/or radical alienness to the other/out-group.[12] (See Box 1.) By reducing people to mere things, anything becomes possible. SS *Obersturmbannführer* Adolf Eichmann, one of the chief organizers of the Holocaust, was not just not thinking— as Hannah Arendt famously argued— but he was not-thinking about non-humans.[13] He was a bureaucrat manipulating numbers and symbols on paper. That's the limit of negative empathy— reducing the other to something non-human— then indeed, everything becomes possible.[14]

By implication, even if Nozick's call for redemption sounds just a tad too religious for your preferences, his (implicitly) suggested link between empathy and atrocity is not that far-fetched. Perhaps we do not need compassion (and other kinds of empathy) to *redeem* ourselves, but we certainly need it to avoid recurrence of the Holocaust

---

11 Slavenka Drakulić, *The Balkan Express: Fragments from the Other Side of the War* (New York: Norton, 1993), 145.

12 Lajos Brons, "Othering, an Analysis," *Transcience: A Journal of Global Studies* 6.1 (2015): 69–90.

13 Arendt, *Eichmann in Jerusalem*.

14 Simon Baron-Cohen suggests to substitute the term "empathy erosion" for "evil," and argues that "empathy erosion arises from people *turning other people into objects*". Baron-Cohen, *The Science of Evil: On Empathy and the Origins of Cruelty* (New York: Basic Books, 2011), 6.

Box 1: The Other / Othering

In her introduction to *The Second Sex,* Simone de Beauvoir wrote that "the category of the Other is as fundamental as consciousness itself" and that "no group ever defines itself without simultaneously positing the Other facing itself."[15] The focus of her book was on women as Other. Throughout most of history women have been depicted as weak, passive, irrational, emotional, and so forth, and men have defined themselves in opposition to that. In *Orientalism,* Edward Said showed that the self-identification of the West *contra* the East takes place in nearly identical terms.[16] Such processes of unequal identity construction are called "Othering."

Othering is the identification of one's own group in opposition to others or other groups in such a way that one's own group turns out to be superior. Constructing the other as inferior or backward justifies exclusion and oppression. However, the main purpose of such unequal identity construction is self-affirmation. People need a more or less positive self-image, and the easiest way to achieve that is to construct one's own identity and the identity of the social groups one belongs to as superior.[17]

and to end the history of (in-)human atrocity. Unfortunately, we are moving in the opposite direction: rather than compassion, *cultural psychopathy* is spreading. And the consequences thereof do not just include atrocities, but also the ongoing destruction of environments, communities, countries, and almost everything else most of us care about.

Of course, I'm not claiming that "psychopathy" explains everything that is wrong in the world. Nor am I dismissing or even devaluing the many acts of compassion that occur and have occurred in any age. What I will be arguing in this essay is that psychopathy *as a cultural phenomenon* is one of the most destructive forces in the history of mankind, and that this cultural psychopathy has become "hegemonic," which has important implications for any attempt at a remedy.

15 Simone De Beauvoir, *Le Deuxième Sexe* (Paris: Gallimard, 1949), 18. My translation.
16 Edward Said, *Orientalism* (New York: Pantheon Books, 1978).
17 See, for example, Fritz Heider, *The Psychology of Interpersonal Relations* (New York: Wiley, 1958), and David K. Sherman and Geoffrey L. Cohen, "The Psychology of Self-Defense: Self-Affirmation Theory," *Advances in Experimental Social Psychology* 38 (2006): 183–242.

Before proceeding to substantiate these claims (in the following chapters) it should be noted that my claim is closely related to Jean Twenge and Keith Campbell's claim that narcissism has become epidemic.[18] Narcissism shares most of its diagnostic indicators with psychopathy (see next chapter), and a cultural trend becoming epidemic is more or less a consequence of its being hegemonic (see the chapter "Hegemony"). Nevertheless, I disagree with both terms in Twenge's and Campbell's cultural "diagnosis." Firstly, the diagnosis "narcissism" is itself symptomatic for what they and I are diagnosing: it focuses too much on the self, thus downgrading how selves relate to others (i.e., empathy). Secondly, the term "epidemic" falsely suggests that this is a natural phenomenon and obscures its political dimension. The hegemony of psychopathy is as much a political as a cultural phenomenon. And even if *my* political preferences are somewhat left of center, the hegemony of psychopathy is not just a problem for the left. Psychopathy as a cultural phenomenon also conflicts with the teachings of all of the "World Religions," and because it destroys community, it should concern the communitarian right as much as it should concern the left. Consequently, although the hegemony of psychopathy is *also* a political problem, it is not a problem for particular political ideologies or organizations— it is a problem for mankind.

18   Jean M. Twenge and W. Keith Campbell, *The Narcissism Epidemic: Living in the Age of Entitlement* (New York: Atria, 2009).

2

Psychopathy

This is obviously not an essay in clinical psychology or forensic psychiatry, and it should be equally obvious that when I write about "psychopathy as a cultural phenomenon" I am not using the term "psychopathy" in its clinical sense.[1] Nevertheless, my use of the term is not unrelated, and to explain what I mean by "psychopathy" it is useful to look at the clinical use of the term first.

Research on psychopathy is dominated by Hervey Cleckley and Robert Hare. The first more or less defined the modern understanding of the disorder in *The Mask of Sanity.*[2] The second converted Cleckley's case-study-based construct into something that can actually be measured and tested by means of his *Hare Psychopathy Checklist.*[3] Cleckley listed 21 (in 1941) or 16 (in 1976) characteristics of the psychopathic personality, on the basis of which Hare developed a checklist to score 20 items. By means of factor analysis

---

1   It can be debated whether there is such a thing as "psychopathy in its clinical sense." Psychopathy is not listed as such in recent editions of the *Diagnostic and Statistical Manual of Mental Disorders* (DSM), but as "antisocial personality disorder." The existence of widely accepted diagnostic criteria does seem to imply that there is a clinical notion of psychopathy, however. See Robert D. Hare, *The Hare Psychopathy Checklist — Revised*, 1st and 2nd edns. (Toronto: Multi-Health Systems, 1991 and 2003).

2   Hervey Cleckley, *The Mask of Sanity: An Attempt to Clarify Some Issues about the So-Called Psychopathic Personality,* 1st and 5th edns. (St. Louis, MO: Mosby, 1941 and 1976).

3   Robert D. Hare, "A Research Scale for the Assessment of Psychopathy in Criminal Populations," *Personality and Individual Differences* 1.2 (1980): 111–19, and Hare, *The Hare Psychopathy Checklist — Revised.*

Table 2: Four Factors of Psychopathy

	Factor / Dimension	*Items*
I	affective	lack of empathy; lack of remorse or guilt; shallow affect; failure to accept responsibility
2	interpersonal	glib / superficial; grandiose self-worth; pathological lying; manipulative
3	lifestyle	stimulation seeking; impulsive; irresponsible; parasitic; lack of realistic goals
4	antisocial	early behavior problems; juvenile delinquency; poor behavioral controls; criminal versatility; revocation of conditional release
	(unrelated items)	promiscuous; many short-term relations

(a statistical technique to reveal underlying "factors" in data) 18 of those 20 are grouped into four factors, shown in Table 2. These four factors can be interpreted as different but not independent dimensions or aspects of psychopathy.

In Hare's first explorations based on Cleckley's 16 characteristics, he found that a factor aggregating lack of empathy, pathological egocentricity, and other characteristics similar to the items in factor 1 in Table 2 was by far the most important (i.e., explained most of the variance). This suggests that the affective factor / dimension is the most central aspect of psychopathy. However, in later studies it is not consistently the case that the affective factor is the most important, but it seems plausible that this is largely due to the fact that psychopathy is almost exclusively researched by forensic psychiatrists and that virtually all of the research samples consist entirely of criminal offenders and / or forensic psychiatric patients, which probably are somewhat atypical (in comparison to the general population) with regards to lifestyle (factor 3) and antisocial behavior (factor 4). The forensic background of Hare's checklist is also clearly reflected in the items of factor 4, antisocial behavior, which focus strongly on criminal behavior. Other kinds of antisocial behavior exist, of course, and a more general (i.e., non-forensic) understanding of psychopathy needs to take that into account. Furthermore, research by David Cooke and his colleagues suggests that antisocial behavior is probably merely a secondary symptom or consequence of psychopathy, and the other factors are more central to the construct.[4] These considerations and findings suggest that the four factors or dimensions differ in their centrality or peripherality to psychopathy: the affective dimension (1) is the most central, followed by the interpersonal and lifestyle dimensions (2 and 3) while the antisocial dimension (4) is a more peripheral aspect.

Most personality disorders are scales or spectra rather than dichotomies,[5] and this is the case for psychopathy as well.[6] By implication, Hare's checklist and its associated psychopathy construct posit a more or less arbitrary cut-off point: patients who score at or above that cut-off on the test are diagnosed with psychopathy, while those who score lower are not. Such a cut-off point or threshold is set at a certain level in accordance with the purpose of the test and construct. In case of Hare's checklist, that purpose is primarily forensic, but in other contexts lower or higher thresholds may be more useful or appropriate, and if the purpose of the construct is not diagnostic (i.e., not applied to individual human beings) then no sharp cut-off may be needed at all. Thus, if one is not so much interested in psychopathy as a predictor of criminal behavior, but as a social or cultural phenomenon, for example, then the threshold should be lowered and blurred sufficiently to pick out levels of psychopathy that pose no serious criminal threat, but that are socially destructive nevertheless. Alternatively, the positing of a threshold can be waived altogether, leaving the concept of psychopathy intentionally vague. People, then, are psychopaths *or not* to differing extents. If some definition of psychopathy is neither a diagnostic tool nor a measuring rod, no arbitrary cut-off point is needed. Therefore, it is this option that I will adopt here.

4   David J. Cooke, Christine Michie, Stephen D. Hart, and Daniel A. Clark, "Reconstructing Psychopathy: Clarifying the Significance of Antisocial and Socially Deviant Behavior in the Diagnosis of Psychopathic Personality Disorder," *Journal of Personality Disorders* 18.4 (2004): 337–57.

5   Lee Clark, "Assessment and Diagnosis of Personality Disorder: Perennial Issues and an Emerging Reconceptualization," *Annual Review of Psychology* 58.1 (2007): 227–57.

6   Robert D. Hare and Craig S. Neumann, "Psychopathy as a Clinical and Empirical Construct," *Annual Review of Clinical Psychology* 4 (2008): 217–46.

Table 3: The Affective Dimension of Psychopathy

Essential Indicators	Additional Indicators
lack of empathic concern	lack of empathic distress
lack of ability or willingness to engage in perspective taking and projection	lack of ability or willingness to engage in simulation
lack of remorse or guilt	failure to accept responsibility

As mentioned, of the four dimensions of psychopathy, the fourth, antisocial behavior, is either peripheral or even a consequence of the other dimensions. Moreover, as non-criminal forms of antisocial behavior are less easily captured in a small list of indicators, I will ignore this dimension. Of the remaining three dimensions, the affective dimension is the most important, and therefore should play a central role in a definition of psychopathy. (See Table 3.) Within this dimension, "lack of empathy" is the most important aspect (it has a factor loading of 0.82, which is the highest of all factor loadings, other factors included). As we have seen before (see previous chapter), the concept of empathy is very ambiguous, however, and consequently, some clarification is needed.

It is possible that a psychopath is deficient to varying extents in all eight kinds of empathy distinguished in the table in the previous chapter, but that doesn't mean that all eight deficiencies would be defining criteria.[7] Hare uses the term "callous" as an alternative denotation for "lack of empathy," which implies that it is a lack of *empathic concern* that is a defining feature. However, in most cases, this lack of empathic concern is probably paired to a lack of empathic distress and (both are) causally related to a lack of ability or willingness to engage in perspective taking, projection, and possibly also simulation. While all of these deficiencies are indicators of psychopathy, some are more essential to the concept than others. Something similar seems to be true for the other items in Hare's checklist: lack of remorse or guilt is a more important indicator (i.e., has a much higher factor loading) than failure to accept responsibility. Table 3 summarizes the indicators of the affective dimensions of psychopathy, taking this difference into account.

---

7   Many psychopaths are good "mind-readers," implying that they have no deficiencies with regards to cognitive empathy.

Table 4: The Interpersonal and Lifestyle Dimensions of Psychopathy

Indicators of the Interpersonal Dimension	*Indicators of the Lifestyle Dimension*
egocentric (grandiose self-worth)	(short term) stimulation seeking, impulsive
glib / superficial	risk-taking, irresponsible
manipulative	lack of realistic (long term) goals
deceitful	parasitic

The other two dimensions require less clarification, although in a few cases a slight change of terms may broaden their applicability. For example, in some variants of Hare's checklist, the more general— and for that reason preferable— term "deceitful" is used instead of "pathological lying." In case of the lifestyle dimension, it needs to be noted that many of the indicators mentioned are hard to separate from each other. Short-term orientation, stimulation seeking behavior, risk-taking, and several of the other indicators mentioned are all closely related. This also includes the "parasitic" indicator, although that may be less obvious. Psychopaths take risks, but intelligent and not-so-intelligent psychopaths take different kinds of risks. That is, intelligent psychopaths take risks on behalf of others, and are parasitic in that sense: if all goes well, the profit is theirs, but if things go wrong, most of the damage is done to others.

Definitions

A psychopath is defined here (i.e., in this book) as someone who matches all of the essential indicators in the left column of Table 3, at least some of the additional indicators in the right column of Table 3, and at least some of the indicators in Table 4. This definition, as mentioned above, is intentionally vague in the sense that it does not posit an arbitrary cut-off point. Instead, it takes explicitly into account that psychopathy is a spectrum: the more indicators apply to some individual, the more psychopathic that person.

This notion of psychopathy is broader and fuzzier than the clinical concept measured by Hare's checklist. It does include psychopaths in that clinical sense, as well as much of the other two, closely related personality disorders in the "dark triad," narcissism and Machiavellianism, but it probably also includes most of the people Eric Schwitzgebel calls "jerks," and which he defines as follows: "the jerk culpably fails to appreciate the perspectives of others around him, treating them as tools to be manipulated or idiots to be dealt with rather than as moral and epistemic peers."[8] In this definition of jerks we find some of the hallmarks of psychopathy as defined above, and some of those that do not appear explicitly in Schwitsgebel's definition of "jerk" appear elsewhere in his text: lack of empathic concern, failure of perspective taking, grandiose self-worth, manipulative. All that is missing is impulsiveness and risk-taking— and on that ground Schwitzgebel argues that jerks are not psychopaths[9]— but those are not essential criteria in the definition of "psychopath" adopted here. It can, of course, be argued that for that reason or from a technical (or dogmatic?) point of view, the broader and fuzzier notion should be called something like "subclinical psychopatoid personality" rather than "psychopathy,"[10] but that would be rather cumbersome, and besides, as long as it is clear that the context of this essay is not forensic psychiatry, the slightly broader understanding of the concept should cause little confusion.

Regarding that context, I wrote above that the topic of this essay is "psychopathy as cultural phenomenon," and I haven't yet said anything about what I mean by that. A distinction needs to be made between *individual psychopathy,* defined above, and *cultural psychopathy,* or "psychopathy as cultural phenomenon." Psychopathy in the latter sense is a disorder of cultures or societies rather than individuals, although the two disorders are closely related. *Cultural psychopathy is the acceptance or even approval by some culture or social group of individual psychopathy as* normal *rather than deviant; it is the normalization of individual psychopathy as defined above.* Wherein "normal" and "normalization" should be read both in their ordinary sense as common and accepted, and in their more technical sense as being in accordance with the norm.

---

8   Eric Schwitzgebel "A Theory of Jerks," *Aeon Magazine,* June 4, 2014, ¶6.
9   Schwitzgebel, "A Theory of Jerks," ¶7.
10 Gary Olson suggests "culturally acquired empathy-deficient disorder having its root in the dominant socioeconomic system" for a very similar notion. *Empathy Imperiled: Capitalism, Culture, and the Brain* (New York: Springer, 2013), 57.

To avoid misunderstanding, it must be emphasized that cultural psychopathy does not necessarily imply a proliferation of psychopaths (even as defined here). In a psychopathic culture psychopathy has become a norm, but even if everyone acts more like a psychopath under the influence of that norm, it doesn't have to be the case that significantly more people become full-fledged psychopaths. Psychopaths are outliers, and an increase in the average (i.e., the average level of psychopathy) does not automatically produce more outliers.

Signs of Cultural Psychopathy

Probably the most conspicuous symptom of cultural psychopathy is the proliferation of psychopaths in movies and TV drama. Examples are easy to find: Tom Ripley (books by Patricia Highsmith and several movie adaptations), Patrick Bateman (*American Psycho* by Bret Easton Ellis), Gregory House, MD (*House*), James Bond, Dexter Morgan (*Dexter*), Sherlock Holmes (as played by Benedict Cumberbatch), and so forth.[11] Nearly every action hero (or anti-hero) in a Hollywood movie satisfies all of the essential and most of the additional criteria of psychopathy identified above, but movie heroes are not the only psychopathic role models in our culture. Over half a century ago, David Hamilton pointed out that "the Entrepreneur takes on the qualities of a cultural hero who performs the miracles of production,"[12] but since then the entrepreneur has been knocked off his pedestal by managers and financial specialists. While—according to Hamilton— the entrepreneur derived his heroic status partly from his creativity, current cultural heroes such as corporate executives and investment bankers derive their status merely from

[11] On Ripley and Dexter, see Kenneth Saltman, "Learning to be a Psychopath: The Pedagogy of the Corporation," in *Critical Pedagogy and Global Literature: Worldly Teaching,* eds. Masood Raja, Hillary Stringer, and Zach Vandezande (New York: Palgrave MacMillan, 2013), 47–62. On House, Bond, and several other "dark triad" characters, see Peter K. Jonason, Gregory D. Webster, David P. Schmitt, Norman P. Li, and Laura Crysel, "The Antihero in Popular Culture: Life History Theory and the Dark Triad Personality Traits," *Review of General Psychology* 16.2 (2012): 192–99.

[12] David Hamilton, "The Entrepreneur as Cultural Hero," *The Southwestern Social Science Quarterly* 38.3 (1957): 250.

performing the "miracle" of shareholder value maximization at all costs. (However, these current cultural heroes are much more controversial than the heroes of the past: they are despised as much by some people as they are revered by others.)

In an interview with Joel Bakan, Robert Hare suggested that the modern corporation has the characteristics of a psychopath.[13] Indeed, corporations are manipulative, risk-taking, incapable of empathy or remorse, and so forth. (It should be stressed that what is true of the vast majority of large corporations is not necessarily true for many smaller businesses, mainly because the latter tend to be much more personal and more embedded in communities.) Corporations are not humans, however, and thus not psychopaths in a strict sense, but their managers and executives *are* human, and are forced and/or expected to behave like psychopaths in their corporate roles. They may even be legally obliged to do so. As Hare points out, that doesn't mean that they *are* psychopaths (although some of them may be): outside the corporation most of them lead normal (i.e., non-psychopathic) lives. Nevertheless, the corporation promotes cultural psychopathy in at least two ways. Firstly, even if corporate executives (etc.) lead double lives, it is in their psychopathic, corporate roles that they are heroes. In other words, they are cultural heroes *as* psychopaths. And secondly, the corporation provides an environment for the cultivation and practice of psychopathic behavior.

If Hannah Arendt is right, then Adolf Eichmann was not a psychopath, but merely a very mediocre bureaucrat who unthinkingly and uncritically did his job within a psychopathic system.[14] Christopher Browning's research on German Reserve Police Battalion 101, which systematically executed thousands of Jews in Poland, reveals a similar unthinking adherence to duty and uncritical acceptance of circumstances.[15] Something similar applies to corporate executives. Of course, I do not want to suggest that environmental disasters

---

13 Joel Bakan, *The Corporation: The Pathological Pursuit of Profit and Power* (New York: Free Press, 2004).

14 Hannah Arendt, *Eichmann in Jerusalem: A Report on the Banality of Evil* (New York: Viking, 1963). See previous chapter.

15 Christopher R. Browning, *Ordinary Men: Reserve Police Battalion 101 and the Final Solution in Poland* (New York: HarperCollins, 1998), especially 72.

and exploitation of workers are comparable to the Holocaust; that's not the point. The point is that the combination of a psychopathic system or institution with bureaucrats or executives performing their roles without ever stopping to think or question what they are doing is a recipe for disaster. It has proven to be.

After the Second World War, territorial growth became an unacceptable ambition for states, but an alternative was found in economic growth: the economy became the primary concern of politics.[16] This change of focus had several important consequences. Most obviously, the absolute prioritization of economic growth over everything else meant and means that in the end only money matters. Culture, education, the environment, and everything else that matters to most people is only of secondary importance at best, and a wasteful distraction at worst. Thus, while territorial ambitions lead to war, economic ambitions lead to environmental disaster and cultural impoverishment, among others.

Secondly, the shift of focus elevated economics to official state doctrine and economists to official suppliers of plans and policies, and the effects thereof on the "science" of economics and on society itself can hardly be exaggerated, but this is a topic that will have to wait until the next chapter. And thirdly, it made the corporation the paradigm of wealth creation, and thereby the fountainhead of economic growth— that is, of the realization of the economic ambitions of the state. From a historical perspective this is somewhat peculiar given that the existence and rise of the modern corporation is the result of a series of historical accidents,[17] but more important in the present context is the establishment of an institutional environment that promotes psychopathic behavior as a paradigmatically desirable institutional arrangement. In other words, the psychopathic work environment became the norm: it is how things should be. And not just in the perspective of the state, because the state's ambitions— through processes discussed in the

16 Timothy Mitchell, "Fixing the Economy," *Cultural Studies* 12.1 (1998): 82–101.

17 Hamilton, "The Ceremonial Aspect of Corporate Organization," *American Journal of Economics and Sociology* 16.1 (1956): 11–24, and Bakan, *The Corporation.*

THE HEGEMONY OF PSYCHOPATHY

next chapter— gradually became society's ambitions, and the state's heroes, moneymakers, became society's heroes— that is, *our* heroes.

It is no wonder, then, that many children growing up with these heroes, with the role models provided by Hollywood and the corporate world (and the former is part of the latter, of course), enter adolescence and adulthood "ethically broken." In "Broken when Entering," Robert Giacalone and Marc Promislo discuss the baggage college students carry into class— that is, the baggage society loads them with.[18] This baggage consists of a mind-set that disparages virtue, demonizes those in need of help, and stigmatizes goodness. Our students "come to us believing that virtuous individuals are dangerous to material goals and should be castigated."[19] Virtues are (or may become) obstacles to the bottom line, and are thus to be avoided or discouraged. Empathy endangers profitability, and is therefore wrong. In the workplace, there is no room for ethics and empathy— psychopathy has become the norm.

But mind-sets are hard to contain, and it is easy to discern the devaluation of goodness, of empathy, and of care everywhere in society. Child-care, nursing, care for the elderly, and so forth are underrated and underpaid, for example, and a ruthless banker, lawyer, or CEO enjoys much more prestige than someone who gives care. So much more, in fact, that if prestige would be quantified, the prestige of care-giving professions would be measured in negative numbers. Non-professional forms of care are similarly devalued and belittled (and usually left to women).[20] Cultural psychopathy turns caring / empathy from a virtue into a weakness, but also into an act of subversion. Empathy / care *must* be devalued, because the very existence of empathy denies the belief in the "naturalness" of egocentricity that the hegemony of psychopathy relies on.

---

18 Robert Giacalone and Mark D. Promisto, "Broken When Entering: The Stigmatization of Goodness and Business Ethics Education," *Academy of Management Learning & Education* 12.1 (2012): 81–101.

19 Giacalone and Promisto, "Broken When Entering," 92.

20 See also Box 1 in the first chapter, and Box 5 in the last chapter.

3

Hegemony

In his *Prison Notebooks,* written between 1929 and 1935, the Italian Marxist philosopher and politician Antonio Gramsci argued that the state's or ruling elite's control over the people can be maintained by two and only two means: coercive power and hegemony. Hegemony is the people's spontaneous consent to and adoption of the values, desires, ideas, beliefs, perspectives, knowledge claims and so forth that serve the interests of the state and/or ruling elite.[1] Although the term "hegemony" was used by other Marxists before, Gramsci's theory is based on the work of Machiavelli more than on that of Marx and his followers.[2] Gramsci explicitly refers to Machiavelli's metaphor of the centaur, for example. The centaur's animal side represents the state's violent side: its control through force and coercion. The centaur's human side represents the state's civilized side: its control through the spontaneous consent of hegemony (see Figure 1.)

In the simplest possible terms, Gramsci's Machiavellian idea is that Jane can make John do what she wants him to do by two and only two means. Either John accepts Jane's power/authority and follows her instructions, or Jane forces him by means of violence or the threat of violence. The first of these is hegemony. Hence, hegemony is the (spontaneous) acceptance of (and/or consent to) the

1 Antonio Gramsci, *Selections from the Prison Notebooks* (New York: International Publishers, 1971), 12.

2 Derek Boothman, "The Sources for Gramsci's Concept of Hegemony," *Rethinking Marxism* 20.2 (2008): 201–15, and Benedetto Fontana, "Hegemony and Power in Gramsci," in *Hegemony: Studies in Consensus and Coercion,* eds. Richard Howson and Kylie Smith (New York: Routledge, 2008).

socio-political status quo— that is, of the existing power/authority relations. (See Box 2 on the notions of power and authority.) Obviously, force and hegemony do not exclude each other. Most likely Jane's power/authority over John would be based on a mixture of threat (i.e., force) and acceptance (i.e., hegemony). Gramsci recognizes this, but also points out that hegemony is the most important of the two because even when force is necessary, that use of force itself needs to be socially accepted (i.e., it needs hegemony).

> The "normal" exercise of hegemony...is characterized by the combination of force and consent, which balance each other reciprocally, without force predominating excessively over consent. Indeed, the attempt is always made to ensure that force will appear to be based on the consent of the majority, expressed by the so-called organs of public opinion....[3]

Furthermore, the use of force is costly and can easily lead to discontent— thus eroding acceptance/consent— if its use is not socially accepted. For these reasons it is difficult— if not impossible— to build a stable state on brute force alone. Rather, as Gramsci argues, a state (or ruling elite) is and should be founded on (the creation of) a worldview.

To avoid misunderstanding, two related clarifications are in order. Firstly, the theory of (cultural) hegemony does not imply that the "ruling elite" is a well-defined, monolithic block with clear and unchanging membership. Rather, membership of the ruling elite is usually gradual and context-dependent— that is, people (and organizations, perhaps) are members of the ruling elite to various degrees and those degrees differ from context to context. Hence, the ruling elite is a much more diffuse and unstable social structure than that term may seem to suggest, and for that reason it is probably a good idea to adopt another term wherever more neutral phrases like "the dominant groups" are less appropriate. "Hegemony" derives from Greek "hegemon" (ἡγεμών) meaning leader, but since the ruling elite is not a singular individual, the plural form of that word, "hegemones" (ἡγεμόνες), may be more appropriate. Therefore, I will (occasionally) use that term below. Once more, the *hegemones*

3 Gramsci, *Selections from the Prison Notebooks,* 80.

Figure 1: A Less Humanoid Centaur

Control through hegemony isn't necessarily as "civilized" or humane as Machiavelli's centaur analogy suggests, and much more pervasive. The "centaur" in this figure better captures those aspects of Gramsci's theory. (Illustration: Ka Ketelmug, 2016.)

(or dominant groups) are neither organized nor strictly separate from the rest of society, but that doesn't make them any less real. (In the same way that the vague boundary between a chunk of pumpkin and its surrounding pumpkin soup doesn't make that chunk any less real. See also Box 4 below.)

Secondly, hegemony is (usually) not planned or actively organized—it is not some kind of conspiracy. (And of course, it *cannot* be if the hegemones are not organized.) Rather, hegemony is a more or less automatic social process. Gramsci suggests that the "spontaneous consent" is caused by the prestige and confidence that the socially dominant group(s) (i.e., the hegemones) enjoy(s), but also that "the intellectuals" and the "organs of public opinion" play an essential role in spreading the worldview of the ruling group(s) to the ruled. A few decades later, Max Horkheimer and Theodor Adorno argued for something very similar in their *Dialectic of Enlightenment*.[4] With the term "culture industry" they

4   Max Horkheimer and Theodor W. Adorno, *Dialektik der Aufklärung* (Amsterdam: Querido, 1947).

Box 2: Power / Authority

It is not entirely clear whether hegemony is the acceptance of power or of authority. The main source of this ambiguity is that the notions of power and authority are ambiguous or even "essentially contested" themselves.[5] Authority and power are often contrasted in terms of rights and abilities: authority is a *right* to get some desired effect, while power is an *ability* to get it, regardless of opposition.[6] As a right, authority depends on acceptance (or recognition, acknowledgment, consent, etc.) of that right: authority is *created* by acceptance (and thus existentially dependent thereon). Power, on the other hand, is objective fact. Power may seem to be dependent on compliance (or obedience), but compliance does not create power. Rather, power conceptually implies compliance, and the other way around—they are different sides of the same coin. Acceptance and compliance stand in different relations to authority and power, respectively, but also point at a further difference: authority is a right to have something *accepted*; power is an ability to have something *done*. To have power over someone means to be able to make that person *do* something. To have authority over someone means having one's judgment that something is true, right, or desirable accepted. Power can be coercive, but one cannot be coerced to think something, only to do something; not to accept some claim, but only to say or pretend that one accepts it. By implication, authority cannot be coercive. From these considerations it can be inferred that "hegemony" refers both to the acceptance of authority of those in power, and to the acceptance of their use of— and right to— power.

referred to the commercial manufacturing, packaging and distribution of a certain perspective on reality. Through its products, such as movies, music, and other forms of commercial entertainment

5   See, for example, Steven Lukes, *Power: A Radical View* (Basingstoke, UK: Palgrave Macmillan, 1974). The contestation of "essentially contested concepts" is essential to the debates they are used in. Each party in the debate claims that their definition is correct, and by implication, there are no neutral definitions. Rather, any definition of an essentially contested concept is normative and political because it captures the interpretation of only one party in the debate. See W.B. Gallie, "Essentially Contested Concepts," *Proceedings of the Aristotelian Society* 56 (1956): 167–98.

6   The most prominent exception is Hannah Arendt, who in "On Violence" argues for a concept of power that is very close to Gramsci's concept of hegemony. See also the first footnote of the next chapter. Hannah Arendt, "On Violence," in *Crises of the Republic: Lying in Politics; Civil Disobedience; On Violence; Thoughts on Politics and Revolution* (New York: Harcourt Brace Jovanovich, 1972), 101–98.

and infotainment, the culture industry largely determines how we perceive and understand the world around us. This was probably a development that Gramsci could not foresee in the 1930s, but due to the spread of new media and the commercialization of news and other kinds of information, the culture industry became the primary hegemony-spreading force. And like hegemony itself, the culture industry is not organized— or at least not with the explicit aim or purpose of spreading hegemonic values and beliefs. Rather, the beliefs and values of the culture industry itself are shaped by hegemony. The dominant group(s) provide(s) the paradigms of success and prestige, but in addition to this influence through visibility and dominance, there tend to be financial relations between the hegemones and the culture industry as well, and as the Dutch saying goes, "whose bread one eats, whose word one speaks."

The hegemonic spread of ideas cannot be openly organized or coordinated. Hegemony is *spontaneous* consent— not coerced acceptance— and depends for its success on invisibility. Hegemony reaches maximum effectiveness when the hegemonic values and beliefs do not need to be supported or promoted anymore; when it becomes unnecessary to say that "there is no alternative" (one of Margaret Thatcher's favorite slogans), because everyone already "knows" that there is no alternative, because the very idea of an alternative has become incomprehensible. David Harvey, Mark Fisher, Tariq Ali,[7] and others have argued that neoliberal capitalism has become hegemonic in this sense.[8] For example, Fisher writes that "the lack of alternatives to capitalism is no longer even an issue" because "capitalism seamlessly occupies the horizons of the

---

7   David Harvey, *A Brief History of Neoliberalism* (Oxford, UK: Oxford University Press, 2007), Mark Fisher, *Capitalist Realism: Is There no Alternative?* (Winchester, VA: Zero Books, 2009), and Tariq Ali, *The Extreme Centre: A Warning* (London: Verso, 2015).

8   Notable earlier pronouncements of the hegemonic character of neoliberal capitalism include Michel Foucault's lectures of 1978–79, *The Birth of Biopolitics: Lectures at the College de France, 1978–1979* (New York: Palgrave Macmillan, 2008), and also Antonio Negri, *The Politics of Subversion: A Manifesto for the Twenty-First Century* (Cambridge, UK: Polity Press, 1989), and Fredric Jameson, *Postmodernism; or, the Cultural Logic of Late Capitalism* (Durham, NC: Duke University Press, 1991).

thinkable."[9] Similarly, Fredric Jameson reports that "someone once said that it is easier to imagine the end of the world than to imagine the end of capitalism."[10] On the other hand, Wolfgang Streeck doesn't just imagine the end of capitalism, but predicts it and offers a compelling argument in support of that prediction.[11]

The current hegemony can be described either as neoliberal or as cultural-psychopathic. To a large extent the difference is one of focus: describing the current hegemony as one of neoliberal capitalism means focusing on the economic and the political; describing it as a hegemony of psychopathy means focusing on the cultural. Many critics of the hegemony of neoliberal capitalism are well aware of the cultural (i.e., psychopathic) aspects thereof. Tariq Ali, for example, points out that Margaret Thatcher's "ideological offensive" was intended to break down the notion of society and associated social consciousness, and replace it with self-centered individualism and consumerism, and that this offensive was successful, leading to a "profound shift in consciousness," in effect leading to the normalization of psychopathy (although Ali does not use that term).[12]

Nevertheless, that the current hegemony can be described either as neoliberal or as psychopathic does not imply that these are just two faces of the same coin or that they necessarily come together. Neoliberalism depends on— but also promotes— cultural psychopathy, and consequently, it is doubtful that the hegemony of neoliberalism could survive a hypothetical demise of the hegemony of psychopathy, but the converse is not the case. The hegemony of psychopathy can— and probably *will*— survive the collapse of the hegemony of neoliberalism (and it may be the case that that collapse is already in process), because culture changes much slower than economic and political institutions.

Among the pillars that support and reinforce the current hegemony— that of psychopathy and neoliberal capitalism— some are more important than others, and different "pillars" play different

---

9 Fisher, *Capitalist Realism,* 8.
10 Fredric Jameson, "Future City," *New Left Review* 21 (2003): 65–79.
11 Wolfgang Streeck, "How Will Capitalism End?" *New Left Review* 87 (2014): 35–64.
12 Ali, *The Extreme Centre,* 5.

roles in the (re-)production and enforcement of hegemonic values and beliefs. Education, for example, is most important in the long run by training future citizens in "spontaneous" consent, while the media and culture industry are more important for the short term spread and reinforcement of hegemonic ideas. In addition to this difference between long and short term effects there is also a difference between more direct and more indirect aspects of hegemony. Hegemony enables and strengthens the ruling elite's control *directly* by manufacturing consent (or acceptance, at least), and *indirectly* by disseminating hegemonic values and beliefs— that is, the beliefs that support the interests of the hegemones. Nevertheless, most pillars of hegemony have both direct and indirect roles, and both long term and short term effects.

Aside from the media and culture industry, among the most important supporting pillars of the current hegemony are mainstream economics, the (self-)corruption of critique, and education.[13] In the following four sections, I will briefly discuss (aspects of) the roles of these key pillars in maintaining and promoting hegemony.

The Mass Media and the Culture Industry

The culture industry and mass media expose its consumers to a continuous stream of exercises in desensitization and dehumanization of which the aforementioned proliferation of psychopaths in movies and TV drama is but one conspicuous manifestation.[14] Psychopathic heroes are the apex of a general and only slightly more subtle glorification of other-disregarding self-interest.[15] In the typical story line, the main or even only function of the protagonist is getting what *she* wants, regardless of the costs for others (that is, the supporting characters), whose interests matter little, if they are presented as having interests at all. The purpose of the others is merely to make the protagonist's story more interesting, but towards that

13 An emerging fifth pillar is control through technology, such as smartphones and the "internet of things."
14 See the section "Signs of Cultural Psychopathy," in the previous chapter.
15 See also Jean M. Twenge and W. Keith Campbell, *The Narcissism Epidemic: Living in the Age of Entitlement* (New York: Atria, 2009), on what they call "the narcissism epidemic": the rise of over-inflated senses of self and of self-centeredness.

end their humanity is denied— the others are nothing but story elements, one-dimensional obstacles (or resources) on the protagonist's self-serving path, disposable *things*, not people.

The products of the culture industry typically divide the world into protagonists and others, and those others are not worth the protagonists' or the audience's empathy; they are outside the scope of empathy. The others are *always* outside the scope of empathy. *That* is the essence of "othering;" *that* is part of what made the Holocaust possible (see the first chapter). One cannot feel empathic concern (or compassion) for someone *and* make that person suffer at the same time. One cannot feel empathic concern for someone who is suffering *and* not want that suffering to end. But take away empathic concern, put the other outside the scope of empathy, and everything becomes possible (as Slavenka Drakulić remarked):[16] violence, rape, murder, the Holocaust. And indeed, Hollywood movies abound with violence against the others.[17] (Video games might also be good— or possibly even better— examples of this, but because I don't know anything about video games, I'll leave the analysis of their contribution to the hegemony of psychopathy to others.)

In dividing the world into protagonists and disposable, dehumanized others, the culture industry propagates a picture of the world that normalizes and justifies the pursuit of private, even selfish goals, while turning a blind eye to others. What the culture industry— through the protagonists of its products— advocates is a lifestyle characterized by a lack of empathic concern, a lack of perspective taking, egocentrism, stimulation seeking behavior, and a general disregard for others.[18] That is (cultural) psychopathy.

16 "I understand now that nothing but 'otherness' killed Jews, and it began with naming them, by reducing them to the other. Then everything became possible. Even the worst atrocities like concentration camps or the slaughtering of civilians in Croatia or Bosnia" (also quoted in chapter 1), Slavenka Drakulić, *The Balkan Express: Fragments from the Other Side of the War* (New York: Norton, 1993), 145.

17 Much more can — and should — be said about the role of violence in the products of the culture industry and in our cultures themselves, but I will not do so here. Brad Evans and Henry A. Giroux, *Disposable Futures: The Seduction of Violence in the Age of Spectacle* (San Francisco, CA: City Lights, 2015), is an interesting recent attempt to address the issue.

18 There are exceptions, of course, especially some TV programs and books

While there are differences between "pure" entertainment and infotainment, the boundary between those is vague and somewhat arbitrary, and infotainment such as news is as obsessed with violence, and as guilty of massive othering as movies and TV drama. Other peoples, minorities, refugees, the homeless, and everyone else who doesn't belong to the in-group is routinely "othered"— that is, dehumanized, represented as a mere thing rather than as a fellow human being with interests, thoughts, and concerns of her own. Such othering plays an important role in maintaining hegemonic control. Othering simultaneously dehumanizes and devalues the others, and affirms the superiority of the in-group. But thereby it also strengthens identification with that in-group and acceptance of that group's values, beliefs, and social structures— that is, hegemony.

The most important function of infotainment, the press and / or the media in maintaining and promoting hegemony, however, is manufacturing consent through the selection of information. As already mentioned above, the media are not immune from hegemony. Rather, under hegemonic influence, the media— mostly unconsciously— pick, twist, and spread "information" and ideas in accordance with the hegemonic values and beliefs. This does not mean, of course, that some particular newspaper or TV channel cannot have an agenda of its own. It does mean, however, that the less explicit that agenda is, the greater the influence of supposedly non-ideological and neutral "common sense," but "neutrality" and "common sense" are just synonyms for the dominant values and beliefs, for hegemony.

There is a persistent myth that the media have a left-wing bias. What feeds this myth is the fact that many producers of news and journalism indeed have (or had) an ideological agenda of their own. But that agenda is (or was) not a left-wing agenda. Rather, much of the media has (or had) a *liberal* bias,[19] but despite the common

aimed at young children that seem to be intended to instill different values.

19 The media landscape has shifted so far to the right in the past decade that — with some notable exceptions — little discernible liberal bias is left. Rather, most of the mass media have a very *aliberal* bias, incorporating elements of nationalism, xenophobia, conservative populism, and cultural psychopathy. But most of all, the vast majority of media organizations are firmly wed to hegemony.

equation by Americans of "liberal" and "left," those two terms do not denote the same thing. Liberalism advocates personal freedom and free choice in the political, economic, and other spheres of life. Liberalism champions free markets, free choice of marriage partner (i.e., same or different sex), political freedom, and so forth. And because it advocates personal freedom and individualism, it opposes oppression and discrimination based on (supposed) group membership, such as sexism and racism. Liberalism (also) espouses values and beliefs that conflict with more traditional, religious, or communitarian belief systems, and moreover, there is some overlap between liberal goals and values and common goals and values of the left. The misidentification of "left" and "liberal" is, therefore, quite understandable. Nevertheless, there are significant differences between the two. For example, not all of the left favors individualism (or at least not to the same extent), not all of the left opposes all traditional values and beliefs, and most of the left does not advocate (completely) free markets (or even explicitly rejects free markets). There is an overlap between parts of the left and liberalism, but the two are certainly not identical.

What's more important, however, than the misidentification of the (former) liberal bias of the media as a left-wing bias, is the role this bias plays (or played). It is important to notice that free market ideology is the *official* ideology of the hegemony of psychopathy (even if in practice large corporations demand state support and other measures that counter free markets). Liberalism is perfectly suitable as the respectable face of neoliberalism, as the attractive wrapping of a poisonous gift. Hegemony is flexible enough to use other ideologies— such as conservatism, authoritarianism, nationalism, or even socialism— for justification and to gain and keep popular acceptance or support.[20] Hegemony doesn't *need* liberalism, but the liberal defense of individualism, personal freedom (in principle, not necessarily in practice), and free markets (idem) is a perfect fit with the values, beliefs, and interests of the hegemony of psychopathy. Moreover, there is one more reason why liberalism is

20 If liberalism proves to be insufficiently popular among the masses, then hegemony will *have* to rely on other ideologies to manufacture consent. A mixture of authoritarianism and nationalism appears to be the first choice in most countries. See also the epilogue.

hegemony's favorite political ideology: it assumes and propagates the same image of man as mainstream economics, and that image— as will be argued below— is an image of man as psychopath.

There is no left-wing bias. The left wants to change the world. The left wants alternatives. Hence, the left wants what according to hegemonic beliefs is impossible. And the mass media almost invariable side with hegemony, rather than with the left. As Tariq Ali remarked: "the media denounces, in sometimes hysterical tones, any alternative that challenges the status quo, however mildly."[21]

Mainstream Economics

The aforementioned reorientation of political ambitions after the Second World War from power and territory to wealth changed the relation between economics and the ruling elite.[22] The "science" of economics, which already had been more influential and prestigious than any of the other social sciences, now gained an effective monopoly as the official supplier of government plans and policies, putting it in the center of power, and changing its status and what was (and is) expected of it. For one thing, politics demand(ed) "closure"— that is, models that give clear and determinate answers— and the economics profession was and is happy to supply. However, closure requires simplification, and consequently, one can *either* have closure and determinacy *or* applicability to the real world. As Joseph Schumpeter remarked in 1930, when it comes to economic questions, one can choose either simple answers or useful answers, but one cannot have both.[23] Lured by power and prestige, economics chose simplicity and closure and gave up realism, and hid that behind rhetoric. (For a sketchy overview of the field of economics and its various schools, see Box 3.)

---

21 Ali, *The Extreme Centre*, 136.
22 See the section "Signs of Cultural Psychopathy" in the previous chapter.
23 Joseph Schumpeter, "Preface," in Frederik Zeuthen, *Problems of Monopoly and Economic Warfare* (London: Routledge, 1930), vii–xiii. See also Erik S. Reinert, *How Rich Countries Got Rich ... and Why Poor Countries Stay Poor* (London: Constable, 2007), and Yanis Varoufakis, *Economic Indeterminacy: A Personal Encounter with the Economists' Peculiar Nemesis* (London: Routledge, 2014).

The two most fundamental simplifications made by mainstream economics are methodological individualism, which treats all human beings as strictly separate and autonomous agents, and the assumption that these autonomous agents always try to maximize the satisfaction of their own, individual, given preferences. The first of these two simplifications implies that communities, power relations,[24] social networks, and most forms of mutual support and cooperation are outside the scope of analysis. It implies that *society* is outside the scope of economic analysis. The second implies among others that human motivations and other aspects of psychology as well as the nature and desirability of (particular) preferences are outside the scope of analysis. Together, these two simplifications result in a model of man that is often dubbed "*homo economicus.*"

It must be emphasized that there is no inherent problem with such simplifications in science. Rather, it is doubtful that science would even be possible without simplification. Accurate prediction requires (usable) models, and models require abstracting away distracting properties. Hence, simplification is a methodological choice that makes modeling— and thus prediction— possible. All theories in physics, for example, abstract away the properties that are (mostly) irrelevant in the given context. To calculate the gravitational pull between two material objects, all you need to know is their masses and distance. However, the properties that are abstracted away in the calculation of gravitational pull re-appear in other physical theories and models, and if a physicist would want to predict the trajectory of some moving object, she would combine various theories and models, and thus various or even all properties. Size and shape, which do not figure in the gravity calculation, enter the picture when friction is taken into account, for example. In other words, simplification or abstraction in physics is really just separation of properties into different partial theories that are to be recombined for accurate prediction.

Simplification in mainstream economics is of an entirely different nature, however. What it abstracts away— human psychology, for example— *never* re-enters the picture. Mainstream

---

24 On the role of power in economics and economies see Norbert Häring and Niall Douglas, *Economists and the Powerful: Convenient Theories, Distorted Facts, Ample Rewards* (London: Anthem, 2012).

Box 3: Schools of Economics

The academic discipline of economics is divided into orthodox and heterodox schools. Orthodox or *mainstream* economics is "neo-classical," which means that it accepts a certain methodology based on abstraction and mathematical formalization. Heterodoxy within economics is not a single school, but a loose cluster of schools including behavioral, institutional, and evolutionary economics, but possibly also economic history and other areas in the overlap with adjacent social sciences. These heterodox schools reject excessive abstraction and formalization, and study actual economic behavior (in the case of behavioral economics), the role of culture and behavioral patterns and habits (in institutional economics), and so forth.

While there are many prominent heterodox economists (such as Thomas Piketty) and mainstream economics is far less visible for a casual observer, the latter has been uncontested as the one and only *official* economic doctrine for at least four decades, even if deviation from that orthodoxy is routinely allowed if it benefits the hegemones themselves.[25] This section only deals with the hegemonic role of mainstream (i.e., orthodox, neo-classical) economics, and completely ignores heterodox economics, for the simple reason that the latter plays no significant role in the hegemony of psychopathy.

economics— in this respect— is like a physics that abstracts away shape, size, and composition in *all* of its theories and models. There is no such physics because it is useless: it cannot predict anything, and even its explanatory power is severely limited. But the exact

25 In most industrialized countries, economic policy is not just determined by neo-classical economics, but also by a much older, more empirical tradition according to which national wealth depends on manufacturing industry more than on trade. This idea motivates policies aimed at fostering innovation and supporting key industries (against neo-classical advice). While the rich countries became rich thanks to such policies they prevent developing countries from implementing similar policies. As Erik Reinert remarks, "in countries like the USA politicians saw to it that the [neoclassical / mainstream] theory was not used if it went against the interests of their own country. Pragmatism ruled at home, and high theory ruled abroad" (*How Rich Countries Got Rich*, 123). See also Ha-Joon Chang, *Kicking away the Ladder* (London: Anthem 2002), Chang, *Bad Samaritans: Rich Nations, Poor Policies, and the Threat to the Developing World* (London: Random House Business, 2007), and Reinert and Arno M. Daastøl, "The Other Canon: The History of Renaissance Economics," in *Globalization, Economic Development and Inequality: An Alternative Perspective,* ed. Reinert (Cheltenham, UK: Edward Elgar, 2004), 21–70.

same thing is true of mainstream economics and for the exact same reason: it cannot predict anything and its explanatory power is close to zero.

Furthermore, simplifications and abstractions in science are justified only if they help to reveal and / or explain the workings of some aspect of reality, but the particular simplifications chosen by mainstream economics— especially in combination with the demand for closure— only succeed in *obscuring* social and economic reality. Moreover, they do not just lack scientific justification, but are inherently ideological as well. They preclude the modeling and analysis of any alternative for neoliberal capitalism, and thereby also make systemic analysis of capitalism itself impossible. With the given simplifications, capitalism is the only possible economic reality. In the introduction to a collection of papers on the artificial suppression of indeterminacy in mainstream economic models, Yannis Varoufakis writes that the two simplifications and the demand for closure are

> tantamount to a decree that every single mainstream economist accepts capitalism as a "natural" system. Consequently, what we are left with is a profession churning out technical studies of fictitious markets which act as mere diversions from the real task of studying capitalism. Of course, the utility of this feat— for those who have an interest in keeping capitalism out of serious theoretical scrutiny— is immense. Capitalism appears in the public's eyes as a complex entity no less natural than the physical universe; it is, we are told, an entity to be analyzed with the clinical impartiality of a social physicist, exploited by financial engineers, tamed by "independent" Central Bankers, and only occasionally criticised by a few superannuated mainstream economists.[26]

And consequently, mainstream economics is "an ideologically driven pseudo-science whose power comes from successfully hiding, as opposed to revealing, the true nature of our social, political and economic relations."[27] (For a well-written, non-academic

26 Varoufakis, *Economic Indeterminacy,* 17.
27 Varoufakis, *Economic Indeterminacy,* xxiv. See also Häring and Douglas, *Economists and the Powerful,* and Michael Hudson, "Technical Progress and

analysis and refutation of some of the most widespread myths that resulted from this, see Ha-Joon Chang's *23 Things They Don't Tell You about Capitalism.*[28])

Mainstream, neoclassical economics has been under fire for well over a century.[29] For example, in 1898 Thorstein Veblen compared *homo economicus* to:

> a lightning calculator of pleasures and pains, who oscillates like a homogeneous globule of desire of happiness under the impulse of stimuli that shift him about the area, but leave him intact. He has neither antecedent nor consequent. He is an isolated, definitive human datum, in stable equilibrium except for the buffets of the impinging forces that displace him in one direction or another.... He is not the seat of a process of living, except in the sense that he is subject to a series of permutations enforced upon him by circumstances external and alien to him.[30]

A chorus of critical voices has joined Veblen in scrutinizing aspects of mainstream economics, its assumptions, and its methodology,

Obsolescence of Capital and Skills: Theoretical Foundations of Nineteenth-Century US Industrial and Trade Policy," in Reinart, *Globalization, Economic Development and Inequality*, 100–11.

28 Chang, *23 Things They Don't Tell You about Capitalism* (London: Penguin, 2010). Other recommended books exposing the myths and fallacies of mainstream economics include John Quiggin, *Zombie Economics: How Dead Ideas Still Walk Among Us* (Princeton, NJ: Princeton University Press, 2010) and John Weeks, *Economics of the 1%: How Mainstream Economics Serves the Rich, Obscures Reality and Distorts Policy* (London: Anthem, 2014). The first of these is aimed at a more academic audience, while in case of the second, the anger is dripping from the pages. I could easily extend this short list of suggestions as there is a vast literature arguing against the obfuscations of mainstream economics. One may wonder why this "vast literature" has so little influence on mainstream thought (in and outside of economics), but the answer to that question should be obvious by now: it is hegemony.

29 If one counts the criticism of classical economics by the German Historical School in the 1840s, for example, then mainstream economics has been under fire for much longer. However, while classical economics has much in common with neoclassical economics, they are by no means identical in their assumptions and methodology.

30 Thorstein Veblen, "Why Is Economics Not an Evolutionary Science?" *The Quarterly Journal of Economics* 12.4 (1898): 389–90.

apparently quieting down a bit in the 1980s and 1990s, only to re-emerge in 2000 when a group of French economics students started the Post-Autistic Economics movement that grew into the main platform for criticism of mainstream economics.[31] Most of main-stream economics dismissed or ignored its detractors, however, and continued on its way unscathed.

Occasionally, a representative of the mainstream responds to some of its critics, however. For example, in a recent paper Don-ald Katzner distinguished "valid" from "invalid" criticism, which is "essentially irrelevant"[32] because it does not "evidence an under-standing of, and fully recognize the real nature, purpose, and inten-tion of that which is being criticized."[33] What he appears to mean with that— judging from the rest of his paper— is that he wants to disqualify any critique of the aforementioned two simplifications and the principle of closure because those *define* the field of eco-nomics as *he* perceives it. The response is typical. Simplification and closure are defended with the *truth* that abstraction is necessary in science, and criticism is brushed aside as lacking understanding of how science— and thus economics— works. But what mainstream economists apparently fail to see is the dis-analogy between their approach and abstraction in, for example, physics. Abstraction in physics is contingent and context-dependent, and physics never loses sight of the fact that in the end *all* relevant properties must be (and will be) taken into account. Mainstream economics, however, abstracts away all aspects of reality that it cannot fit in its mathemat-ical universe, *and then forgets about them*. Mainstream economics is like a biology that abstracts away multicellular organisms because it can only model unicellular life, and then pretends to be able to analyze and predict *all* life on the basis of that model. It's not the

---

31 In 2008 it changed the title of its flagship journal from *Post-Autistic Economics Review* to *Real-World Economics Review,* after it was realized that the label "post-autistic" is both insulting (to people with autism, not to mainstream economists) and incorrect. The movement is still known under its original name, however.

32 Donald W. Katzner, "A Neoclassical Curmudgeon Looks at Heterodox Criticisms of Microeconomics," *World Economic Review* 4 (2015): 63–75; 63.

33 Katzner, "A Neoclassical Curmudgeon Looks at Heterodox Criticisms of Microeconomics," 64.

critic of such a biology (or such an economics) who evinces a lack of understanding of how science works (or should work, at least).

Furthermore, the apologists of mainstream economics are not just blind for the methodological inappropriateness of non-contingent simplification (i.e., for never returning from abstraction to the real world), but also for the implications thereof. That is, mainstream economists are themselves the firmest believers in the dogma that a kind of capitalism characterized by unbridled competition is the only possible reality, but that dogma is the consequence of abstracting away society, cooperation, mutual support, and everything else that makes us human. Hence, it is a dogma founded in illegitimate abstraction, rather than in reality.

Katzner's paper shows what many critics of mainstream economics already knew: that criticizing its most basic choices and assumptions is taboo. As Varoufakis observed, the economics profession "works like a priesthood, dedicated solely to the preservation of its dogmas".[34] (Or, in the words of John Weeks, "the role of [mainstream economics] in society is as a religious sect with an extremely doctrinaire priesthood that zealously guards its doctrines".[35]) The dogmatic blindness reaches nauseating levels in Katzner's warning that "invalid criticisms can have serious consequences if damaging policy decisions eventually emerge from them".[36] Heretics are dangerous, he tells us, with the confidence of a true believer.

From the late 1970s onward the World Bank and IMF forced the developing world to adopt economic policies based on mainstream economic dogma. These policies destroyed infant industries and decimated real wages and economic growth. Nowhere in the developing world did neoclassical economic policy reduce poverty. Countries that did develop quickly— like the East-Asian "tigers"— did so mostly because they protected their industries *against* economic dogma. Most of Africa isn't poor because *critics* of mainstream economics gave them bad policy advice, but because mainstream economists forced them to follow a path of economic destruction.[37] And

34 Varoufakis, *Economic Indeterminacy,* xxiv.
35 Weeks, *Economics of the 1%,* 17.
36 Katzner, "A Neoclassical Curmudgeon Looks at Heterodox Criticisms of Microeconomics," 64.
37 Chang, *Kicking away the Ladder,* Chang, *Bad Samaritans,* Reinert, *How*

consequently, the refugees that risk their lives in an attempt to reach Europe or the US are really political refugees, fleeing the poverty and lack of prospects forced upon them by the West's neocolonial policies.[38] The destructive influence of mainstream economics hasn't been limited to developing countries, however. The European economic crisis— and especially the economic problems of Southern Europe— are largely due to the "Hunger Games" policy based on mainstream economic dogma as well.[39]

More than 7 million children die each year from poverty, hunger, and preventable diseases. They die in countries that could have seen economic growth, food security, and better medical institutions, if it wasn't for the mainstream economists' (of IMF and World Bank) demands to open up their markets and destroy their infant industries. Probably not all developing countries could have followed the same path as South Korea, for example, but with more sensible economic policies— like they had *before* economic destruction was forced upon them— most of them would have had industrial growth and economic growth, enabling better healthcare, better education, better infrastructure, starting a virtuous cycle of growth and development. It's difficult to give an exact number, but it seems a *very* conservative estimate to say that in such a scenario the yearly number of children dying from poverty, hunger, and preventable diseases would be (much) less than half of what it is now. And that

Rich Countries Got Rich, and Reinert, "Neo-classical Economics: A Trail of Economic Destruction Since the 1970s," *Real-World Economics Review* 60 (2012): 2–17.

38   The British Empire did not allow its colonies to develop a manufacturing industry and destroyed (most notably in India) whatever manufacturing industry there was. This policy was copied by the other colonial powers, and preventing colonies from developing themselves by denying them manufacturing industry and any other kind of economic activity that could start a virtuous circle of growth (and forcing them to focus on agriculture, mining, and so forth) became a defining feature of colonialism. Given that the policies that are forced upon the "developing" world nowadays have the exact same effect, colonialism has never ended.

39   Servaas Storm and C.W.M. Naastepad, *Macroeconomics beyond the NAIRU* (Cambridge, MA: Harvard University Press, 2012), and Storm and Naastepad, "Europe's Hunger Games: Income Distribution, Cost Competitiveness and Crisis," *Cambridge Journal of Economics* 39.3 (2015): 959–86.

would imply that mainstream economics is responsible for the death of approximately 100 million children since 1980.

And that's "just" children, and only in the developing world. A meta-analysis by Sandra Galeo and colleagues suggests that in 2000 more than 800,000 Americans died of poverty-related causes.[40] If adding up numbers of deaths is insufficient, then add, for example, the massive environmental destruction resulting from abstracting away the environment from mainstream economic models, or the deterioration of job satisfaction due to treatment of workers/employees as disposable resources rather than as human beings (or as *homines economici*, which is just as inhuman), and it becomes clear that mainstream economics has been one of the greatest evils in history.

And Katzner warns us of the *critics* of mainstream economics...

While the foregoing may explain (some of) what's wrong with mainstream economics, it doesn't really say anything about its role in maintaining and promoting hegemony. That role is threefold. Firstly, it provides the economic policies that enrich the hegemones, thus maintaining or even reinforcing the economic base of their power. Secondly, it gives the hegemonic belief that "there is no alternative" the air of "scientific fact." And thirdly, it promotes cultural psychopathy.

Hegemony is a process of consent-generation, and the most effective way of generating consent to some social arrangement is to make people believe that that arrangement is natural and that there is no real alternative. That— as argued above— is exactly what mainstream economics does, and the importance thereof can hardly be overstated. Mainstream economists are the high priests of the hegemony of psychopathy.

As explained above, mainstream economics' picture of man, *homo economicus,* embodies its most fundamental dogmas, but that picture is a picture of a psychopath. Of the essential indicators of the affective dimension of psychopathy (Table 3 in the previous chapter) and the indicators of the interpersonal and lifestyle dimensions

40 Sandra Galeo, Melissa Tracy, Katherine J. Hogatt, Charles DiMaggio, and Adam Karpati, "Estimated Deaths Attributable to Social Factors in the United States," *American Journal of Public Health* 101.8 (2011): 1456–65.

of psychopathy (Table 4) there isn't a *single* indicator that does *not* apply to *homo economicus*. He (or it?) is a psychopath by any standard, and thus, if mainstream economics successfully promotes that picture, then it promotes psychopathy. As it turns out, it does have such effects indeed. This is the "third role" of mainstream economics in maintaining hegemony mentioned above: the promotion of cultural psychopathy through education and through its influence on language, metaphors, and "common sense."

In the paper "Economics Language and Assumptions: How Theories can Become Self-Fulfilling," Fabrizio Ferraro, Jeffrey Pfeffer, and Robert Sutton summarize a mountain of evidence for the thesis that mainstream economics does not just shape how we perceive social reality, but shapes reality itself.[41] They show how economic theories, metaphors, and language have infected the rest of society, and how those thereby (or as a consequence thereof) have changed society itself. An obvious example of the corrupting influence of mainstream economics is the spread of policies based on mistrust and on the assumption that everyone is only concerned with their own interests. Evidence shows that this assumption is unwarranted, but that it becomes true in certain circumstances: if you treat people as unreliable and egoistic, then that is how they *will* behave;[42] they may even start believing that their behavior *should* be determined by self-interest exclusively.[43]

One of the most interesting parts of Ferraro, Pfeffer, and Sutton's paper is their review of research on the effects of economics education on students.[44] This research shows that exposure to mainstream economic doctrine makes students more self-interested,

---

41 Fabrizio Ferraro, Jeffrey Pfeffer, and Robert I. Sutton, "Economics Language and Assumptions: How Theories can Become Self-Fulfilling," *Academy of Management Review* 30.1 (2005): 8–24.

42 C. Daniel Batson, Jay Coke, M.L. Jasnoski, and Michael Hanson, "Buying Kindness: Effect of an Extrinsic Incentive for Helping on Perceived Altruism," *Personality and Social Psychology Bulletin* 4.1 (1978): 86–91, and Samuel Bowles, "Policies Designed for Self-Interested Citizens May Undermine 'The Moral Sentiments': Evidence from Economic Experiments," *Science* 320.5883 (2008): 1605–9.

43 Dale Miller, "The Norm of Self-Interest," *American Psychologist* 54.12 (1999): 1053–60.

44 Ferraro, Pfeffer, and Sutton, "Economics Language and Assumptions," 14.

more deceitful, more manipulative, less empathic, less likely to feel guilt or remorse, and so forth. (And more recent research confirms this.[45]) In other words, it makes students match (many) more of the indicators of psychopathy.[46] It may not change them into full-blown psychopaths, but psychopathy comes in gradations, and there is ample evidence that "education" (or indoctrination) in the dogmas of mainstream economics makes students more psychopathic.

The (Self-)Corruption of Critique

Hegemony is the spread of ideas (such as values and beliefs) that support and maintain the socio-political status quo. Therefore, alternative sources of ideas may undermine hegemony, but if hegemony is effective, then alternative ideas may not be taken seriously, or may even undermine themselves. If hegemony is effective, then the belief that there is no alternative becomes common sense, turning proposed alternatives (for common sense) into obvious nonsense. This is how hegemony undermines critique: by making it "irrational." (A special case hereof is the medicalization of discomfort and dissent, but although important, that topic is outside the scope of this essay.[47]) Critique can also undermine itself in various ways, however, helping hegemony to do "its job," and it is not always easy to determine whether certain corruptions of critique were the product of hegemony or relatively independent developments that just helped hegemony.

The focus here is on the corruption of critical ideas, but hegemony also undermines their social carriers. Under the influence of the hegemonic belief that there is no alternative, most political parties, labor unions, feminist organizations, and so forth that started

45 See, for example, Long Wang, Deepak Malhotra, and Keith Murninghan, "Economics Education and Greed," *Management Learning & Education* 10.4 (2011): 643–60, and Mathias Philip Hühn, "You Reap What You Sow: How MBA Programs Undermine Ethics," *Journal of Business Ethics* 121 (2014): 537–41.

46 See Tables 3 and 4 in the second chapter of this volume.

47 On this topic and other ways in which psychiatry, psychology, and related sciences are used to invalidate discomfort, stifle dissent, and strengthen hegemonic control, see Jacques Davies, *The Happiness Industry: How the Government and Big Business Sold us Well-Being* (London: Verso, 2015).

out as critics gradually but surely moved towards acceptance (or even supporters) of the status quo and the social, political, and economic worldview that supports it. And those who refused to comply were ridiculed (as Utopian lunatics or something similar) and marginalized (with the help of the mass media) or even criminalized.

The main alternative sources of ideas— that is, potential competitors with the hegemonic ideas— are philosophy (in the broadest possible sense of that term) and religion. Throughout history, religion has usually sided with the powerful, however. Rather than opposing hegemony, religion has more often been a tool of hegemony. This is entirely understandable, of course, as religious institutions have been well rewarded for their support of the sociopolitical status quo, but it is also possible that the apparent closeness between religions and the hegemones is partly the result of an evolutionary process: opposing hegemony decreases the chances of survival, and therefore, many religious currents that did so declined or were even wiped out, while those that sided with hegemony grew and ended up dominating the religious landscape. Regardless of such institutional and historical considerations, religion is a potential source of counter-hegemonic ideas, or at least of ideas opposing the hegemony of psychopathy. In all of the "World Religions" compassion is one of the most important virtues (if not *the* most important virtue). Psychopathy is the polar opposite of compassion. Therefore, cultural psychopathy and the hegemony that promotes and spreads it should be the archenemies of all of the World Religions. Although there are religious leaders— including very prominent ones— that regularly speak out against (aspects of) the hegemony of psychopathy (without using that term, of course), in practice religions remain firmly wed to hegemony. This raises the question: Why? Why is this potential source of counter-hegemonic critique so effectively disarmed?

It is easier to focus your attention on "bad" things other people do (such as abortion or marrying people they are not "supposed" to) than to focus your attention on what you do yourself or on what— according to your religion— you should do, especially if hegemony tells you that you're not doing anything wrong. More concretely, all of the World Religions instruct their believers to be compassionate, but it is easy to forget that when hegemony tells you that it is OK to be selfish and religious leaders distract you by means of easier targets that don't mess with your self-image. If this rough sketch is (close to) accurate, then a mixture of institutional factors, hegemony, and the need for self-affirmation all contribute to the undermining of religion as a potential source of critique. And considering that each one of these would probably be powerful enough to do so on its own, it is no wonder that religion is failing as a source of counter-hegemonic ideas (and thereby failing itself).

The second potential source of critique, philosophy, isn't doing any better, unfortunately. Socrates considered his role to be like that of a "gadfly" sent by the Gods to wake up democracy, which he compared to a "well-bred horse that has become sluggish because of its size" and which, because of that, is in need to be roused by critical thinkers.[48] Philosophers, critical theorists, and other thinkers in the same neighborhood may pride themselves by thinking they are gadflies like Socrates (assuming he was one, which is debatable), but in practice they're anything but.

Since half a century or so Western philosophy has been split into two camps that do not communicate with or even understand each other: analytic philosophy (which thrived in the UK and US), and Continental philosophy (which thrived in France and Germany). Analytic philosophy was forced into barren abstraction and away from social relevance during the Cold War and never recovered.[49] This is probably most visible in branches like ethics and social philosophy. Most research in ethics within the analytic tradition, for example, concerns meta-ethics (which focuses on highly theoretical questions about the nature of moral truth, the existence of moral facts, and so forth), and what is left of normative ethics is mostly an elaborate attempt to justify not having to care about other people's suffering.[50] This trend may have reached its apex in the so-called "Ethics of Care" that proclaims that one has moral obligations only to people that one has relations with.[51] The Ethics of Care is

48 Plato, *Apology*, 30e.
49 George Reisch, *How the Cold War Transformed the Philosophy of Science* (Cambridge, UK: Cambridge University Press, 2005).
50 There are exceptions, of course. By far the most prominent among those is Peter Singer. See Peter Singer, "Famine, Affluence, and Morality," *Philosophy and Public Affairs* 1.3 (1972): 542–43.
51 Carroll Gilligan, *In a Different Voice: Psychological Theory and Women's Development* (Cambridge, MA: Harvard University Press, 1982), and Nel

supposed to be an ethics of empathy, but it really is an "ethics" of exclusion, a theory that limits the scope of empathy to one's personal acquaintances. Hence, the "Ethics of Care" is a cynical misnomer— considering that it advocates that one doesn't have to care about the 99.999% or so of the world population that one doesn't have a relation with, the "Ethics of not giving a [insert your favorite swearword here]" would have been a more fitting name.[52]

Continental philosophy and its allies such as critical theory, social studies of science, post-modernist philosophy, neo- (and post-)Marxism, and so forth have not fared much better, but while analytic philosophy as a potential source of counter-hegemonic critique was destroyed by hegemony, Continental philosophy self-destructed. Until fairly recently, virtually all Continental philosophy (broadly understood) adhered to some form of (metaphysical and epistemological) anti-realism,[53] often denouncing realism as "reactionary." But the anti-realist rejection of a reality independent from (or external to) our theories, beliefs, and languages in favor of a radical form of social constructionism implies a rejection of objectivity, and without objectivity there are no objective grounds for critique.

Much of Continental philosophy confuses truth and knowledge with "held to be true" and "socially accepted as knowledge" or similar concepts, but those are not the same notions, and the fact that most of what we hold to be true (i.e., what we believe) and most

Noddings, *Caring: A Feminine Approach to Ethics and Moral Education* (Berkeley, CA: University of California Press, 1984).

52 I'm ignoring Ethical Egoism here because it plays no significant role in philosophy. Ethical Egoism is the moral theory that claims that the only moral obligation one has is to further one's own (objective, long term) interests. Although this theory is the *de facto* ethics of the hegemony of psychopathy and is very popular among the semi-literate fans of Ayn Rand, it is very hard to defend, and for that reason a very uncommon position among moral philosophers.

53 Lee Braver, *A Thing of This World: A History of Continental Anti-Realism* (Evanston, IL: Northwestern University Press, 2007). On the recent emergence of realist (or anti-anti-realist?) Continental philosophy, see Levi Bryant, Nick Srnicek, and Graham Harman, "Towards a Speculative Philosophy," in *The Speculative Turn: Continental Materialism and Realism,* eds. Levi Bryant, Nick Srnicek, and Graham Harman (Melbourne, Australia: re.press, 2011), 1–18.

of what we call knowledge is indeed socially constructed does not imply that reality itself is socially constructed. (See also Box 4.) Giving up the idea of an external/independent reality (in addition to being absurdly anthropocentric) means giving up on the idea of an independent check on our beliefs, and thereby giving up on the notions of objectivity and (objective) truth. But without objectivity (or objective truth), claims cannot be judged by the extent to which they represent the way things are, but only by the interests they serve and by their rhetorical success. The word "truth," then, effectively becomes a euphemism for rhetorical success. Without objectivity, a liar is not misrepresenting reality (because there is no such thing as representing reality) but just an unsuccessful rhetor: lying is failing to convince. (See also next section.) Conversely, telling the "truth" is succeeding; "truth" is rhetorical success; "truth" is power. And therefore, rejecting objectivity and (some form of) realism is opening the door to tyranny.

Where this leads is perhaps best illustrated by Slavoj Žižek who in his writings never offers a transparent argument for his claims, but instead tries to beat his readers into submission with a barrage of rhetorical tricks. Žižek's love of violence is not just textual, moreover, as he pairs the Continental substitution of power/rhetoric for truth/objectivity with a more general adoration of power/violence in the political sphere: Žižek's political aims are best described as the wet dreams of a violent psychopath.[54] In this way, Žižek has effectively become an agent of hegemony, simultaneously disarming counter-hegemonic critique by denying it the only weapon it has— truth— and by infecting it with a psychopathic love of violence, both textual and political.

Suffering, injustice, oppression, poverty, hunger, and so forth are *real.* They are facts. But Continental anti-realism rejects the categories of "real" and "fact"— at least in an objective sense— along with truth and objectivity, and thus, rather than objective fact, suffering (etc.) becomes just a perspective or a social construction. This, of course, is one of the most useful aspects of Continental thought

---

54 On Žižek's violent fantasies, see, for example, Alan Johnson, "Slavoj Žižek's Theory of Revolution: A Critique," in *The Legacy of Marxism: Contemporary Challenges, Conflicts, and Developments,* ed. Matthew Johnson (London: Continuum, 2012), 37–55.

Box 4: Realism and Anti-realism

In some sense, mountains are socially constructed. That is, where we draw the boundary between mountains and hills and around individual mountains (or between mountain and valley) is largely a matter of social convention. That doesn't make the chunks of rock that we refer to with the word "mountain" any less real, however. The anti-realist claim that there *really* are no mountains is as silly as what is often considered its antithesis: the essentialist claim that our word "mountain" picks out a natural kind, meaning that what is mountain and what is not and where and how we draw the boundaries is not a matter of convention, but some kind of natural fact waiting to be discovered. Such essentialism has plagued Western philosophy since Aristotle,[55] and is nowadays often assumed to be an inherent part of realism. Realism—in that view— holds a number of theses that anti-realists reject.[56] These theses, however, are largely independent from each other. One can, for example, hold the "realist" thesis that there is an objective, mind-dependent, external reality, and simultaneously reject the supposedly equally "realist" theses that truth is correspondence with that reality and that there is one and only one true and complete description of how the world is; and there is a small minority of Western philosophers who defend(ed) such inter-mediate positions in between realism and anti-realism.[57] This is not the place to argue for such a view, but I believe that such an intermediate view is right.[58] The anti-realist rejection of the notion of an objective/

55 Throughout most of the history of Western philosophy, essentialism has been the default position. In Analytic philosophy it is stronger than ever since Saul Kripke's *Naming and Necessity* (repr. 1980; Oxford: Blackwell, 1972). In Asian philosophy, on the other hand, essentialism is far less com-mon. Buddhist and Jainist philosophy, for example, are explicitly anti-essen-tialist, and essentialist tendencies are also rare in Chinese philosophy.

56 Two influential lists of theses commonly attributed to realism and suppos-edly rejected by anti-realism can be found in Searle and Braver, written by an analytic and a continental philosopher, respectively. (It must be noted that Searle rejects several of the theses that he identifies as being commonly attributed to realism as "mistakes." See also the next footnote.) See John Searle, *The Construction of Social Reality* (New York: The Free Press, 1995) and Braver, *A Thing of This World*.

57 This includes several very prominent philosophers, such as W.V.O. Quine, Hilary Putnam, Searle, and in some interpretations, Donald Davidson.

58 The beginnings of my argument for such an intermediate position can be found in Lajos Brons, "Dharmakīrti, Davidson, and Knowing Reality," *Comparative Philosophy* 3.1 (2012): 30–57, and Brons, "Meaning and Reality: A Cross-Traditional Encounter," in *Constructive Engagement of Analytic and Continental Approaches in Philosophy,* eds. Bo Mou and Richard Tieszen (Leiden: Brill, 2013), 199–200. For another interesting argument

Box 4: Realism and Anti-realism (continued)

external reality is as implausible as the "realist" (or more appropriately, essentialist) belief that the world comes pre-organized in natural kinds.[59]

from a hegemonic point of view— if there are no objective facts but just social constructions, then there are no facts of poverty or environmental destruction. Unfortunately, naivety prevented many (but not all) Continental thinkers from seeing this consequence of their rejection of "reactionary" realism. It took Bruno Latour, one of the most influential Continental thinkers on science, a few decades to realize this, for example. He awoke from his anti-realist slumber when he found that his ideas are now used to brush aside scientific facts about climate change. And, of course, *now* he is arguing for facts.[60]

Most Continental philosophers will probably consider the foregoing a misrepresentation or caricature of their ideas, and *to some extent* it is indeed. Within social constructionism, more sophisticated and more vulgar strands can be distinguished. Vulgar constructionism is relativist and radically anti-realist— it rejects objectivity, facts, and the notion of reality. Hence, the above is— more or less— a representation of the Continental mainstream as vulgar constructionism. But very few continental philosophers explicitly defend such vulgar constructionism. The problem, however, is that outside the small circle of (apparent) sophisticated constructionists, social constructionism almost always devolves into vulgar relativism, and that even sophisticated constructionists tend to espouse radical anti-realism in most contexts and only retreat to more sophisticated views when challenged. In other words, the foregoing only misrepresents the self-image of Continental philosophy, not its real face.

relative to an intermediate position between realism and anti-realism called "relative essentialism," see Samuel Wheeler, *Neo-Davidsonian Metaphysics: From the True to the Good* (New York: Routledge, 2014).

59 One reason why the rejection of an external / objective reality is implausible is that the possibility of language and communication seems to depend on the existence of a shared, external reality. See Brons, "Dharmakīrti, Davidson, and Knowing Reality."

60 Bruno Latour, "Why Has Critique Run out of Steam? From Matters of Fact to Matters of Concern," *Critical Inquiry* 30.2 (2004): 225–48.

"The philosophers have only *interpreted* the world in various ways; the point is to *change* it," wrote Karl Marx in 1845,[61] but in the last half century or so, neo-Marxists, post-Marxists, and others influenced by his ideas have even forgotten about *interpreting* the world— let alone changing it— and just interpret *texts.* I imagine that Marx would have been less than pleased by this co-optation of his work by an academic cult specializing in mass-producing a kind of inscrutable, sectarian "theoretical work" detached from all reality and undermining attempts to change the world more than helping them; but these "thinkers" could not have done the hegemones a greater favor.

Education for Compliance

In *Not for Profit,* Martha Nussbaum warns against a kind of (higher) education that is focused only on short term economic interests, and that disparages traditional aims of education such as intellectual autonomy and independence.[62] With special reference to the situation in India, she writes that

> education for economic growth needs a very rudimentary familiar-
> ity with history and with economic fact…. But care must be taken
> lest the historical and economic narrative lead to any serious criti-
> cal thinking about class, about race and gender, about whether for-
> eign investment is really good for the rural poor, about whether
> democracy can survive when huge inequalities in basic life-chances
> obtain…. The student's freedom of mind is dangerous if what
> is wanted is a group of technically trained obedient workers to
> carry out the plans of elites who are aiming at foreign investment
> and technological development. Critical thinking will, then, be
> discouraged….[63]

---

61 Karl Marx, *Thesen über Feuerbach* (1845), in Marx and Friedrich Engels, *Werke,* Vol. 3 (Berlin: Dietz, 1969), 5–7; 7. My translation.
62 Martha Nussbaum, *Not for Profit: Why Democracy Needs the Humanities* (Princeton, NJ: Princeton University Press, 2010). On the (traditional) aims of education, see Roger Marples, ed., *The Aims of Education* (London: Routledge, 1999).
63 Nussbaum, *Not for Profit,* 20–21.

There is a worldwide tendency to convert education into the mass-production of "human resources"— that is, disposable things that can be used in the production process— and to devalue or abolish anything that is not expected (by mainstream economics and their political allies) to contribute to profit and short-term economic growth. Towards that end schools and universities have gradually revised their curricula to focus more on "marketable skills" (to the detriment of the humanities and social sciences), and many have been taken over by managers without any background in education, or have been subjugated to the market by other means. The same business ideology has corrupted healthcare and other public and social services in many countries. While these are important developments, and much more can be said about them, they are merely the *result* of the hegemonic influence of cultural psychopathy, and there are more subtle and less obvious ways in which education plays a role in *maintaining* hegemony.

From a hegemonic perspective, the primary function of education is training future citizens in "spontaneous" consent. As Nussbaum remarked, freedom of mind, critical thinking, and intellectual independence are dangerous and should be discouraged. However, hegemony cannot openly thwart or even disparage critical thinking, because critical thinking and intellectual autonomy are cornerstones of liberal democracy, the official ideology of hegemony. But that only means that hegemony needs the *appearance* of promoting critical thinking. Unsurprisingly then, critical thinking has become a buzzword in education, while what is taught under that header has been hollowed out.

With few exceptions, the teaching of critical thinking in higher education takes one of two forms: either it is offered in the form of an informal logic course, or it is incorporated into a writing course such as "persuasive writing." The former approach is typical wherever philosophy departments— especially those affiliated with analytic philosophy— are in charge of teaching critical thinking. The latter is the typical approach of English departments.[64] Both mostly fail to teach critical thinking, but for very different reasons.

64 Richard Paul, "The State of Critical Thinking Today," *New Directions for Community Colleges* 130 (2005): 27–38. For an influential example of the identification of critical thinking with informal logic, see H. Siegel,

Courses in critical thinking as informal logic focus primarily on discovering flaws in the arguments of others, usually by means of short, fairly abstract examples. The approach appears to be motivated by an assumption that improving one's own thinking (i.e., finding and avoiding flaws in one's own reasoning) automatically follows from learning to scrutinize the arguments of others (if that indeed is what students learn). That assumption stands in needs of a warrant, however. The very purpose of philosophical debate— and arguably, without debate there would be no philosophy— is to point out the flaws in the arguments by others, flaws that the authors did not and could not find themselves. The history of philosophy is a long series of expositions of flaws in arguments and responses in the form of new arguments, and nothing in that history suggests that the ability to expose flaws in others' arguments entails the ability to avoid flaws in one's own.

Furthermore, this approach to critical thinking is inherently passive, which is probably its most useful feature from a hegemonic point of view. The counterpart of the implicit view that critical thinking is nothing but the scrutiny of others' arguments, is that "citizens who make an informed choice between options outlined by authorities have fully exercised their critical capacities," as Laura Kaplan aptly put it.[65]

But that is *not* sufficient. The ability to think critically also implies the ability to question whatever is *behind* the options given (i.e., why those options were given), and to find and scrutinize further options (that were not given). Of course, this is generally acknowledged by advocates of critical thinking as informal logic,[66] but uncovering hidden assumptions is the most difficult and

"Educating Reason: Critical Thinking, Informal Logic, and the Philosophy of Education — Part Two: Philosophical Questions Underlying Education for Critical Thinking," *Informal Logic* 7.2–3 (1985): 69–81.

65 Laura Duhan Kaplan, "Teaching Intellectual Autonomy: The Failure of the Critical Thinking Movement," in *Re-Thinking Reason: New Perspectives on Critical Thinking,* ed. Kerry S. Walters (Albany, NY: State University of New York, 1994), 205–20; 209.

66 See, for example, Sharon Bailin and Siegel, "Critical Thinking," in *The Blackwell Guide to the Philosophy of Education,* eds. Nigel Blake, Paul Smeyers, Richard Smith, and Paul Standish (Malden, MA: Blackwell, 2003), 181–93.

least mechanical aspect of critical thinking and is, for that reason, neglected in critical thinking courses. The consequence is that— at worst— what is left of critical thinking in informal logic courses is a sterile numbering and/or diagramming of arguments and checking them against the list of fallacies, but even at best, actual course content does not extend much beyond this.

Critical thinking as taught by English departments doesn't fare much better, unfortunately, albeit for entirely different reasons. The theoretical or philosophical orientation of most English departments, as well as that of most other language and literature departments, is heavily influenced by the Continental tradition in philosophy (see previous section) and especially by the postmodernist branches thereof, but (usually) shorn of all political content (the latter especially after the Culture Wars of the 1990s). It embraces Continental anti-realism, anti-positivism, and opposition to "grand narratives," while de-emphasizing or ignoring (at least publicly) political critique. For that reason, this theoretical orientation is best characterized as *post-critical.*

What may explain this postmodernist or post-critical orientation is that truth, objective facts, and grand theories do not play an important role in literature, that the anti-realist rejection of any reality beyond "texts" chimes well with the focus and concerns of much of the humanities,[67] and that the implication thereof that there is nothing but rhetoric provides support for the prioritization of rhetoric over analysis in writing courses.

Teaching rhetoric often starts with Aristotle's modes of persuasion: *ethos, pathos,* and *logos*— roughly, the credibility of the rhetor (speaker or writer), the appeal to the emotions of the audience, and the persuasive quality of the argument, respectively. If there is no such thing as objective truth, or getting it right— except perhaps as a misleading metaphor for convincing oneself— then all a writer can rely on is these modes as tools to convince some audience. Then the purpose of proper references and reliable data sources is merely the

---

67 According to Jacques Derrida, there is "nothing outside the text" (*"il n'y a pas de hors-texte"*), but the notion of text here is broader than the ordinary notion and includes — in some interpretations — buildings, movies, works of art, and various other kinds of artefacts. Derrida, *De la Grammatologie* (Paris: Les Éditions de Minuit, 1967).

credibility of the author ("building *ethos*"). Then arguments do not need to be valid or well-supported, and proofs only need to *appear* to be true (and thus even fallacies are not necessarily to be avoided, as long as the audience doesn't notice). And then any manipulative appeal to emotions is allowed, as long as it works.

The general disregard for analytical skills in persuasive writing (and similar) courses is not just a consequence of a post-critical rejection of truth in favor of rhetoric, however. It is also related to the explicit focus on writing (and speaking, in some courses). The consequence of this focus is that a course in persuasive writing is (generally) just that: it teaches how to persuade rather than how to argue, how to convince rather than how to be right. Students do not learn how to analyze arguments or discourses, how to pick up on ideological distortions, or how to detect flaws in reasoning or rhetorical tricks. Critical thinking thus is voided not just of the "critical" aspect, but of "thinking" as well, and degenerates into trying to get one's way.

The demise of critical thinking education is not just the result of disciplinary preoccupations (which are formed partly by hegemonic pressures themselves), however. Financial and political pressures play an equally important role. Political critique threatens the financial security of the school and administrators and politicians often demand political neutrality, and consequently, (controversial) social and political topics are avoided in critical thinking courses (of both varieties). But "neutrality" is never really neutral. As Elie Wiesel pointed out in his Nobel Peace Prize acceptance speech, "neutrality helps the oppressor, never the victim."[68] Neutrality is a euphemism for acceptance of the socio-political status quo, that is, of hegemony.

What passes for teaching critical thinking either implicitly teaches to accept the options given and thereby to accept the authority of who- or whatever gives those options (i.e., hegemony), or shifts away the attention from critical thought to desires and how to satisfy them, thus producing egocentric and manipulative consumers rather than critical thinkers. Either is fine for hegemony, of course; what would be less ideal from a hegemonic point of view

68 "Elie Wiesel–Acceptance Speech," *Nobel Prize*, December 10, 1986, www. nobelprize.org/nobel_prizes/peace/laureates/1986/wiesel-acceptance_ en.html, ¶8.

is a critical thinking course that actually supports intellectual independence (rather than unthinking, "spontaneous" acceptance) and a critical attitude. And considering that intellectual independence is among the main, traditional aims of education, this means that under the hegemony of psychopathy, education fails in achieving its main goals.[69]

Summary of the Foregoing

Cultural psychopathy was defined in the second chapter as the acceptance or even approval by some culture or social group of psychopathy as normal rather than deviant— that is, as the normalization of psychopathy. And (individual, rather than cultural) psychopathy was characterized by a lack of empathic concern, a lack of remorse, egocentricity, and a number of other deficiencies with regards to the willingness and / or ability to take others into account.

My main claim in this essay is that cultural psychopathy is hegemonic, and thereby has become a pervasive aspect of modern culture. The notion of hegemony in this sense was developed by Gramsci on the basis of ideas by Machiavelli and others. The core of Gramsci's theory is that political control can have only two bases: hegemony and force. There are only two ways to make someone do what you want him to do: either he accepts your command, or you force him (by means of violence or the threat of violence, or otherwise). The first is hegemony. Hence, hegemony is the acceptance of and consent to the socio-political status quo. Hegemony works through the spontaneous, uncritical acceptance of the values and beliefs that support that status quo.

Most of the third chapter described aspects of the role of four "pillars" of hegemony in maintaining and promoting the hegemony of psychopathy: the mass media and "culture industry," mainstream (neoclassical) economics, "critique," and (higher) education. The mass media and culture industry promote egocentricity and normalize psychopathy, numb the senses (particularly our sense of empathy) by means of a continuous exposure to violence, and actively spread hegemonic values and beliefs in "news" and infotainment. Mainstream economics promotes a picture of man as psychopath,

69 See Marples, *The Aims of Education.*

67

gives the (false!) hegemonic belief that "there is no alternative" the status of "scientific fact," and makes people and societies more psychopathic through policy and indoctrination. (And in addition to all that, mainstream economics is also responsible for the lack of development in most of the "developing" world, and the consequent suffering, as well as for environmental degradation, among others.) The last two sections (before this one) showed how hegemony effectively undermined critique— often with the help of the "critics" themselves— and impoverishes (higher) education.

These pillars support the hegemony of psychopathy directly by manufacturing and reinforcing consent through "education," news and infotainment, and the continuous repetition of the so-called "realist" mantra that there is no alternative.[70] But they also support the hegemony of psychopathy in a more indirect way by spreading and promoting the values and beliefs that support hegemony on the long term. Particularly, the first two of these pillars actively promote egocentricity and erode empathic concern (by devaluing or even dismissing empathy and care), and all four undermine any kind of nonconformity or dissent.

---

70 Note that this is the "realism" of political realism — or better, *capitalist realism* — not the metaphysical realism discussed in the section on the (self-) corruption of critique. See Fisher, *Capitalist Realism*.

4

The War of Position

The Machiavellian core of Gramsci's theory of hegemony is that a state's socio-political control (i.e., its power) can rest on two and only two bases: "spontaneous" acceptance/consent, and brute force. The term "hegemony" (or "cultural hegemony") refers to the first of these two: to the spontaneous acceptance of and/or consent to the socio-political status quo.

Gramsci's theory has some important implications. First and foremost, if in some state hegemony breaks down, the hegemones can only rely on brute force to remain in control, and the weaker hegemony (i.e., the weaker the acceptance of the hegemones' power/authority), the more force is needed.[1] If the hegemones cannot sufficiently compensate the decline of hegemonic control with force (or if a government is toppled, and the new government has insufficient hegemonic support *and* insufficient access to force), then society may collapse into civil war, especially if there are multiple belief systems competing to take over from the old hegemonic beliefs.

Furthermore, because brute force is costly and most likely to reduce hegemonic support (because people are less willing to spontaneously consent to a regime that is killing them), this implies that

1   Hannah Arendt made a very similar argument in "On Violence," differing mainly in the substitution of the terms "power" and "violence" for Gramsci's "hegemony" and "force." Arendt's concept of power is related to legitimacy and acceptance. If a state loses power — in Arendt's sense of that term — it must and will rely on violence to remain in control. See Hannah Arendt, "On Violence," in *Crises of the Republic: Lying in Politics; Civil Disobedience; On Violence; Thoughts on Politics and Revolution* (New York: Harcourt Brace Jovanovich, 1972), 101–98.

if some group of revolutionaries wishes to take control of a state— and keep it— then it needs to assure that it has sufficient hegemonic support *before* it attempts to take control. This means that before any actual struggle for power can begin, there has to be a struggle against the dominant, hegemonic values and beliefs, and an attempt to replace them— as much as possible— with counter-hegemonic values and beliefs that simultaneously reduce hegemonic support for the current regime and raise support for the new one, waiting to take over. Gramsci called this the "war of position." Only after that phase in the revolutionary struggle has been passed successfully— that is, when the group's counter-hegemonic ideology has found sufficient support— the "war of manoeuvre" in which the revolutionary group actually attempts to gain control can start.

This is one of the most important lessons that any would-be revolutionary or reformer can learn from Gramsci (or Machiavelli): the struggle of ideas *must* precede the struggle for power. It is not a lesson well-learned, however, as many revolutionaries, reformers, and other kinds of political activists appear to be unaware of the power of hegemony in preserving the status quo. (One cannot say they assume that they have already won the "war of position"— because they don't know that term and what it means— but many appear to be acting on that assumption.) Any would-be revolutionary or reformer *must* counter hegemony if the change she wishes to produce conflicts with the hegemones' interests. A sufficiently persistent activist may be able to get some results— as long as it is more opportune for the hegemones to give in to her demands than to resist them— but never will these lead to significant change. Hegemony resists change (except if it is in the hegemones' interest), and without a change in hegemony no significant change is possible. Hence, an environmental activist is deluding herself if she beliefs she can save the planet by focusing on specific environmental problems while ignoring the hegemonic beliefs that caused— and will keep causing— them. And a Muslim, Buddhist, Christian, or Hindu wishing to live in a more compassionate society— that is, a society more in line with the teachings of her religion— is similarly deluding herself if she believes that that is possible without fighting— and defeating— the hegemony of psychopathy. To fight hunger, you have to fight hegemony. To fight poverty, you have to fight hegemony. I can easily extend this list, but the point should be clear

THE WAR OF POSITION

already: except if you're rich and/or powerful and without a conscience, the hegemony of psychopathy is your enemy.

This means, of course, that in the fight against the hegemony of psychopathy— assuming that you're interested in fighting that fight— we'll have many allies, or many *potential* allies at least, if we're able to convince them. The enemies of the hegemony of psychopathy include socialists, anarchists, communitarian conservatives, environmentalists, Buddhists, Muslims, Christians, Hindus, and many more. These are all potential allies.

There is an obvious objection to this claim: all these "potential allies" want different things— why should they even want to cooperate, and what's to prevent them from fighting each other? This objection is mistaken, however. To a large extent, all of these allies (without scare quotes) want the same thing: they want a society that is not just ruled by selfish monetary interests, they want a less psychopathic, more compassionate (or more empathic) society. And the only way to achieve that is to replace the current hegemony that values cultural psychopathy with a new hegemony that values compassion/empathy. (Note that psychopathy is a lack of empathic concern, primarily, and that the negation thereof— i.e., lack of lack of— brings us back to empathy.) Hence, what all these allies want (or should want, at least) is to replace the hegemony of psychopathy with its opposite, with a hegemony of compassion/empathy. Of course, that's not *all* they want: most of them have various aims in addition to defeating the hegemony of psychopathy, aims that can be reached only after such a defeat, but this should be no reason for concern. *If* we are able to defeat the hegemony of psychopathy and make empathy hegemonic instead, *then* we'll be able to listen to and try to understand each other, and try to imagine ourselves in each other's shoes (because that is what empathy means), and then we will be able to work something out.

A Brief Utopian Interlude

There is a large and growing literature proclaiming that more empathy and care will lead to a better world. This literature is the Utopianism of our time. It sells dreams about a better world, without reflecting on the possibility of realizing those dreams, and

Box 5: Gender and Empathy / Care

It is often assumed that women are more caring than men (see also Box
1 in the first chapter in this volume). According to male chauvinists this
makes women more suitable for caring tasks such as childcare and nursing; according to female chauvinists this makes women more suitable
for almost anything.[2] However, if there is scarcity of sufficiently caring / empathic people relative to the number of tasks that require such
people, then it would be socially desirable if those people take up those
tasks. In other words, this kind of female chauvinism may lead to the
exact same conclusion as male chauvinism: women should take care of
children, their families, the sick, and the elderly, and only concern themselves with other tasks after all the caring is done. Hence, the feminist
credentials of female chauvinism are rather dubious.

More important, however, is that both forms of gender chauvinism
are based on a false assumption: there is no evidence that women are
inherently more caring / empathic than men.[3] But there is growing evidence that actually *giving* care makes one more caring / empathic.[4] Giving care leads to hormonal and neurological changes with such effects.
Consequently, insofar as (some) women are more caring / empathic than
(some) men, this is not because of a biological difference, but because of
a cultural difference: forcing women (or people in general) to do more
caring makes them more caring (thus producing and simultaneously
confirming the myth of gender difference).

2   Carroll Gilligan, *In a Different Voice: Psychological Theory and Women's
    Development* (Cambridge, MA: Harvard University Press, 1982), and Sara
    Ruddick, *Maternal Thinking: Towards a Politics of Peace* (Boston, MA:
    Beacon, 1989). See also Iddo Landau, "Good Women and Bad Men: A Bias
    in Feminist Research," *Journal of Social Philosophy* 28.1 (1997): 141–50, doi:
    10.1111/j.1467-9833.1997.tb00369.x.
3   Sara Jaffee and Janet S. Hyde, "Gender Differences in Moral Orientation: A
    Meta-Analysis," *Psychological Bulletin* 126 (2000): 703–26. See also Hyde,
    "The Gender Similarities Hypothesis," *American Psychologist* 60.6 (2005):
    571–92.
4   Anne E. Storey and Toni E. Ziegler, "Primate Paternal Care: Interactions
    Between Biology and Social Experience," *Hormones and Behavior* 77 (2016):
    260–71. Pilyoung Kim, Paola Rigo, Linda C. Mayes, Ruth Feldman, James
    F. Leckman, and James E. Swain, "Neural Plasticity in Fathers of Human
    Infants," *Social Neuroscience* 9.5 (2014): 522–35. Eyal Abraham, Talma
    Hendler, Irit Shapira-Lichter, Yaniv Kanat-Maymon, Orna Zagoory-Sharon,
    and Ruth Feldman, "Father's Brain is Sensitive to Childcare Experiences,"
    *Proceedings of the National Academy of Sciences of the United States of
    America* (PNAS) 111.27 (2014): 9792–97, doi: 10.1073/pnas.1402569111.

without identifying obstacles and enemies of empathy/care (i.e., the hegemony of psychopathy). I have no intention to indulge in similar Utopianism, but the last sentences of the previous section may sound ridiculously Utopian and cry out for an explanation.

An effective hegemony does not just propagate values and beliefs, but also the second-order belief that those (first-order) beliefs are natural, inevitable, or beyond doubt and scrutiny. Consequently, an effective hegemony of psychopathy does not just propagate the pathological egocentricity typical of psychopathy (see the second chapter in this volume), but also the belief that human beings are *naturally* egocentric (and thus that egocentricity is not pathological but normal). The latter doctrine is called "psychological egoism." It is a widespread and influential doctrine— as one would expect of a hegemonic doctrine— but it is also false.

The least defective arguments for psychological egoism succeed in proving that human beings have selfish motives. However, from that intermediate conclusion they then invalidly jump to the claim that human beings *only* have selfish motives. Contrary to this claim, there is a mountain of evidence that human motivation is too complex to be reducible to a single factor.

In his most recent book, the psychologist Daniel Batson distinguishes four kinds of motivation: egoism, altruism, collectivism, and "principlism;" and reviews the evidence for each.[5] Of these four, the first two— egoism and altruism— are particularly strong. Human beings are not just motivated by their own well-being, but also by that of cared-for others. (It is often assumed that there are gender differences in this respect. See Box 5.) "Principlism" is Batson's term for being motivated by moral principles, and is the main topic of his book. He shows convincingly that we *present* ourselves as being guided by principles, but that in practice, almost no one is (because we only need to be *seen* as moral by others). Moral integrity is extremely rare, while moral hypocrisy is very common. In the final chapter of his book he considers ways to make moral integrity more common, assuming that this would be desirable, but that assumption is debatable.

---

5   C. Daniel Batson, *What's Wrong with Morality? A Social-Psychological Perspective* (Oxford, UK: Oxford University Press, 2016).

"Principlism" or moral integrity is being *genuinely* motivated by one's moral principles, but different people have different moral principles, and these may be in conflict. There is no guarantee that if everyone would act according to their moral beliefs, this would actually result in a significantly more habitable world. It may even increase moral conflict.

As mentioned, of the four motivations, "principlism" is the weakest (to the extent of being virtually absent in most people), while egoism and altruism are the strongest. Batson's own research shows that altruism is the effect of empathic concern.[6] Feeling for/with the other makes us care about that other. Batson rejects altruism as a reliable moral motivation because experiments show that it does not always produce fair results,[7] but these experiments only show that if we empathize with only one party involved in some moral dilemma, we unfairly benefit that one party. Hence, what these arguments show is that if we exclude some party from empathic concern, we will act unfairly towards that party, but that is hardly surprising.[8]

What we need, then, is a kind of empathic concern that isn't restricted to just those we already cared about, but that is automatically extended to everyone involved in our decisions, and everyone affected by our actions. Perhaps, we need a different term for that. In ancient Buddhist writings the Pali term "*mettā*"— usually translated as "loving-kindness" or "benevolence"— is used to refer to

---

6   Batson, *Altruism in Humans* (New York: Oxford University Press, 2011).

7   Strictly speaking, Batson does not consider altruism a moral motivation at all because in his terminology only principlism is a *moral* motivation.

8   In *Against Empathy,* Paul Bloom rejects empathy for a number of reasons, but he confuses different notions of empathy (see the table in the first chapter of this book). If we discard his arguments against empathic distress and emotional contagion (or sympathy), which are of little relevance here, then all we are left with is the familiar argument that empathy is always partial, biased, and narrowly focused, and therefore, unlikely to produce fair results. (This is also the basis of my critical note about the "Ethics of Care" in the previous chapter.) This is a valid argument, of course, but I'm not advocating (such narrow) empathic concern as a moral foundation. Rather, my argument is that compassion (i.e., empathic concern) is a social necessity, and that empathy is partial (etc.) does not in any way refute this. Nevertheless, I do believe that empathic concern is also morally relevant, although probably only indirectly, but that is a topic for another essay. See Bloom, *Against Empathy: The Case for Rational Compassion* (London: Bodley Head, 2016).

genuine care for the other's well-being, or to something comparable to the love one feels for one's friends, but without restriction to particular targets. Hence, *mettā* is empathic concern for everyone.[9]

Because empathic concern makes us care about others and take their interests into account, this kind of diffuse empathic concern would make us care about all relevant others and take everyone's interests into account. That— ideally— is what an empathic counter-hegemony should establish. There are no blueprints for such a post-psychopathic future, and neither can there be, but any group of people the members of which *genuinely* care about each other and about each other's interests is able to communicate, cooperate, and compromise. This is what underlies the "Utopian" remarks at the end of the previous section.

Some Tactical Considerations

Nearly everyone *should* want to fight hegemony, but of course, almost no one actually does. The reason is obvious: hegemony. As long as hegemony is effective, only very few oppose it, or are even aware of it.[10] That is the nature of hegemony. The other side of the coin is that the more successful the fight against hegemony and the weaker it becomes, the more people will be able to wake up from their hegemonic slumber and join the fight. The questions "How to fight hegemony?" and "How to get (more) people to join that fight?" have the same answer.

Nevertheless, the question "How to fight the war of position?" is really two questions (at least). It is a question both about tactics and about methods, both about *what* to fight and about *how* to fight. Before returning to the implications of Gramsci's Machiavellian theory of the two bases of control, I will offer some thoughts on both in the following, but no answers, or no complete answers, at least.

---

9   The Sanskrit term that is commonly translated as "compassion" is "*karuṇā.*"
10 It is the nature of hegemony that those who are under its influence are unaware of it. The stronger the hegemonic influence, the weaker the awareness of the workings of hegemony. And by implication, the stronger the hegemonic influence, the stronger the "resistance" to the claims of this essay.

Fighting hegemony, counter-hegemonic activism, or the "war of position" is a struggle for minds, not for political power. Hence, while Srdja Popovic and Matthew Miller's *Blueprint for Revolution,* for example, provides many interesting examples of (and ideas for) political activism, it is largely useless in the fight against the hegemony of psychopathy.[11] Popovic and Miller give suggestions on how to mobilize people against a crumbling hegemony; it starts *after* the war of position is already well advanced or even won. We are nowhere near that stage. A better suggestion on what is needed can be found in Mark Fisher's *Capitalist Realism,* already quoted above: "emancipatory politics must always destroy the appearance of a 'natural order,' must reveal what is presented as necessary and inevitable to be a mere contingency."[12] Again, the war of position is a "war" of ideas, and the most potent weapon in the opponent's arsenal is the idea of the naturalness of the status quo, the idea that there is no alternative. And since the strongest, most systematic support for this idea— this *false* idea— comes from mainstream economics, that must be among our main targets.

That, however, is not the only reason to target economics. As argued above,[13] mainstream economics is at least partially responsible for massive environmental destruction and massive suffering, poverty, hunger, and death, but also for the spread of cultural psychopathy. Mainstream economics harms students, as well as other people under its influence, by making them less empathic and more psychopathic. Mainstream economics provides the hegemones with a justification for the continuation of policies that only serve their interests, while turning everyone else into disposable things. Mainstream economics spreads and continuously reinforces the core hegemonic belief that there is no alternative. Mainstream economics is one of the most destructive, evil forces in the history of mankind. It *must* be destroyed.

11 Srdja Popovic and Matthew Miller, *Blueprint for Revolution: How to Use Rice Pudding, Lego Men, and Other Non-Violent Techniques to Galvanize Communities, Overthrow Dictators, or Simply Change the World* (Brunswick, Australia: Scribe, 2015).

12 Mark Fisher, *Capitalist Realism: Is There no Alternative?* (Winchester, VA: Zero Books, 2009), 17.

13 See the section "Mainstream Economics," in the third chapter of this volume.

Some "heterodox" economists (see Box 3 in the chapter "Hegemony" in this volume) believe that economics as a whole can be reformed, or somehow cured from the cancer that is neoclassical, mainstream economics. However, even if they are right, it is much easier— and therefore, strategically preferable— to target economics as a whole. This may raise worries about "collateral damage," but those worries are unfounded. Insofar as they haven't been banished from the discipline already, heterodox economists (i.e., critics of the mainstream) can find new homes in economic sociology, economic history, economic psychology, anthropology, and geography (while neoclassicists cannot do so because they deny the relevance of society, history, psychology, culture, and space / environment). We don't need a *discipline* of "economics" to have sensible economic ideas (for economic policy, for example)— other branches of the social sciences and humanities can take care of that, and do so with better, less ideologically colored, and more realistic results.[14]

But mainstream economics is only one of the pillars of the hegemony of psychopathy (see the previous chapter), and it certainly is not sufficient to focus all attention there. Economists are the high priests of the hegemony of psychopathy, but in spreading its gospel the mass media and culture industry are at least as important. Among others, the mass media maintain and support hegemony by means of "news" and other infotainment that dehumanizes others (such as refugees, the homeless, people of other nationalities, the unemployed, the sick, the elderly, the poor, and so forth), reducing them to just "other," to faceless abstractions rather than living, breathing people. The culture industry maintains and supports hegemony by means of movies, TV dramas, and video games that glorify self-centeredness, psychopathy, and violence. The media and culture industry expose people to a continuous stream of desensitizing violence and other hegemonic propaganda, but just cutting off that stream is insufficient to counter it: we must take control of the message and show the suffering caused by the hegemony of psychopathy. We must fight numbness and raise compassion.

These are the two most important tactical objectives: destroying mainstream economics, and changing the stream of psychopathic

14 Ha-Joon Chang, *23 Things They Don't Tell You about Capitalism* (London: Penguin, 2010), chapter 23.

propaganda into one that promotes empathy instead. There may be other targets and other tactical goals, but without realizing these two objectives we have no chance of winning the "war." This leads us back to the question of *how* to fight. I don't know the answer to that question, however. My fight is with the third pillar— that of the corruption of critique— primarily, and I don't even know how to do that.[15] Nevertheless, I do have something to say about how *not* to fight.

The Monstrosity of Violence

Nietzsche warned that one "who is fighting monsters has to watch out that he doesn't become a monster oneself."[16] We cannot fight psychopathy with psychopathy. And obviously, we cannot fight the hegemony of psychopathy with means that promote psychopathy— that would be self-defeating. But this means that the fight against hegemony is radically asymmetrical, not just in resources and power, but also in tactics and "techniques." We cannot allow ourselves to dehumanize the enemy, because dehumanization is what we are fighting. We cannot allow ourselves a lack of compassion— *even for the enemy*— because a lack of compassion is what we are fighting. Hence, we have to deny ourselves some "options" that our enemies will not deny themselves; we have to disallow ourselves to do to our enemies what they will do to us. Because otherwise we become the "monsters" we set out to fight. Because otherwise we become the enemy.

It only takes a brief exercise in imagining oneself in the shoes of a victim of violence to realize that this means that we cannot resort to violence. Violence and empathy do not go together. If you can kill— if you can kill the enemy— then you *are* the enemy. Teachers of compassion in the distant past realized this well. This is probably why Jesus instructed his followers to "turn the other cheek"

---

15 For my views on philosophy, see Lajos Brons, "Anarchism as Metaphilosophy," *The Science of Mind* 53 (2015): 139–58.

16 Friedrich Nietzsche, *Jenseits von Gut und Böse: Vorspiel einer Philosophie der Zukunft* [*Beyond Good and Evil*] (1886), §146, my translation. The fragment continues with the much better known sentence, "And when you look in the abyss for too long, the abyss will look back into you."

(Matthew 5:39) and why it is written in the *Quran* that even "if you would stretch your hand towards me to kill me, I will not stretch my hand towards you to kill you" (5:28). But the realization that the monstrosity *of* the enemy can never be an excuse for monstrosity *towards* the enemy also clarifies what exactly makes that enemy "monstrous."

Perhaps, one cannot blame a *clinical* psychopath for not empathizing with his victims for the same reason that you can hardly blame a cat for torturing and killing mice. One can certainly blame a "normal" 10-year-old child for torturing and killing mice, however, and insofar as the fight is against real people rather than against some abstract and amorphous force called "hegemony," those people tend to resemble that 10-year-old child more than the cat. That is, they are not suffering from a psychopathic personality disorder, but are *psychopaths-by-choice.* They *choose* not to empathize with the victims of their actions and decisions, while— contrary to the clinical psychopath— they are perfectly able to do so.[17] Hence, they

---

17   There is evidence that the rich refuse to empathize with people outside their social circle (i.e., members of the middle class, the poor, etc.) and are thus psychopaths-by-choice — see, e.g., Jennifer Stellar, Vida Manzo, Michael Kraus, and Dacher Keltner, "Class and Compassion: Socioeconomic Factors Predict Responses to Suffering," *Emotion* 12.3 (2012): 449–59; Michael Kraus, Paul Piff, Rodolfo Mendoza-Denton, Michelle Rheinschmidt, and Dacher Keltner, "Social Class, Solipsism, and Contextualism: How the Rich are Different from the Poor," *Psychological Review* 119.3 (2012): 546–72; Paul Piff, "Wealth and the Inflated Self: Class, Entitlement, and Narcissism," *Personality and Social Psychology Bulletin* 40.1 (2014): 34–43; and David Dubois, Derek Rucker, and Adam Galinsky, "Social Class, Power, and Selfishness: When and Why Upper and Lower Class Individuals Behave Unethically," *Journal of Personality and Social Psychology* 108.3 (2015): 436–49.
      Evidence that studying mainstream economics makes people more psychopathic suggests that many mainstream economists (who are exposed to the corrupting influence of their theories much more and much longer than their students) are also psychopaths-by-choice; see Fabrizio Ferraro, Jeffrey Pfeffer, and Robert I. Sutton, "Economics Language and Assumptions: How Theories can Become Self-Fulfilling," *Academy of Management Review* 30.1 (2005): 8–24.
      And finally, Robert Hill and Gregory Yousey show that politicians score high in narcissism, which is closely related to psychopathy and also involves limited empathy, but to what extent this lack of empathy is a matter of

decide who is worth their empathy and who is not. It may be tempting to argue that those who choose to exclude others from empathy are not entitled to being empathized with themselves, but that would completely miss the point of the "monstrosity objection" and be self-defeating moreover, because making *that* argument is choosing to exclude psychopaths-by-choice— and thus *some* others— from empathy. It is at that point that one who is fighting monsters becomes a monster oneself.

Nevertheless, the ban on violence needs some qualification. "Violence" is usually understood to mean something like physical force against a person, but in political philosophy and adjacent areas of thought the concept is stretched for political reasons. Both the political right and the left stretch the concept to subsume under it what they perceive to be grave injustices. What motivates this is the assumed inherent badness of violence: if that assumption is granted, then anything that falls under the definition of violence is— by definition— bad, and thus no further argument to substantiate that badness is necessary. The "grave injustices" that (part of) the right and left subsume under "violence" are related to private property and (economic) inequality respectively. Part of the political right stretches the concept of violence to include the use of physical force against what a person owns,[18] thus making theft and arson kinds of violence. Part of the political left, on the other hand, stretches the concept of violence to include the systematic use of political and economic power (rather than physical force) against (groups of) persons,[19] turning many kinds of social injustice into kinds of

choice or inability is unclear (although it seems more likely that politics leads to a decrease in voluntary empathy than that it selects for congenital lack of empathy). See Hill and Yousey, "Adaptive and Maladaptive Narcissism among University Faculty, Clergy, Politicians, and Librarians," *Current Psychology* 17.2 (1998): 163–69.

18 Robert Audi, "On the Meaning and Justification of Violence," in *Violence: Award Winning Essays in the Council for Philosophical Studies Competition,* ed. Jerome A. Shaffer (New York: McKay, 1971), 45–99. C.A.J. Coady, "The Idea of Violence," *Journal of Applied Philosophy* 3.1 (1986): 3–19, doi: 10.1111/j.1468-5930.1986.tb00045.x.

19 Johan Galtung, "Violence, Peace, and Peace Research," *Journal of Peace Research* 6.3 (1969): 167–91. Newton Garver, "What Violence Is," in *Philosophy for a New Generation,* eds. A.K. Bierman and James A. Gould, 2nd edn. (New York: Macmillan, 1973), 256–66, doi: 10.2307/2105905.

violence. We should resist stretching the concept of violence in either direction because these re-definitions are distracting rather than helpful: they divert attention from the reason why violence is wrong.

Empathy can tell you what's wrong with violence— just imagine yourself to be a victim of violence. Why would you say that violence *in that case* (i.e., violence against you) is wrong? Probably because it hurts (physically and/or emotionally) and/or because it causes injury or even death. Causing suffering, injury, or death is wrong. Everyone agrees that suffering, getting injured, or dying is bad. All that empathy adds to this is the realization that it is just as bad if it happens to someone else as when it happens to oneself. Violence is wrong because it dehumanizes by implying that the other is not worthy of empathy, and because it causes suffering, injury, and/or death.

Furthermore, there also is a strategic reason to reject violence: it is (usually) counterproductive. Seeing or hearing about violence, especially violence resulting in death, increases the awareness of our own mortality and activates psychological defense mechanisms that are more likely to strengthen hegemonic beliefs than weaken them. According to Terror Management Theory "the awareness of death gives rise to potentially debilitating terror that humans manage by perceiving themselves to be significant contributors to an ongoing cultural drama," and "reminders of death increase devotion to one's cultural scheme of things."[20] Hence, much of what we (humans) do and believe is driven by "terror management," controlling the fear of death, and "effective terror management is faith in a meaning providing cultural worldview and the belief that one is a valuable contributor to that meaningful world."[21] In other words, reminding people of their mortality— or increasing "mortality salience"— leads them to bolster both their worldviews and their beliefs that they are valuable contributors to the world according to that

---

20 Sheldon Solomon, Jeff Greenberg, and Thomas A. Pyszczynski, *The Worm at the Core: On the Role of Death in Life* (New York: Random House, 2015), 211.

21 Jeff Greenberg and J. Arndt, "Terror Management Theory," in *Handbook of Theories of Social Psychology,* 2 vols., eds. Paul A.M. Van Lange, Arie W. Kruglanski, and E. Tony Higgins (London: Sage, 2012), 1:398–415 ; 1:403.

worldview. This hypothesis is usually called the Mortality Salience Hypothesis and is the most extensively tested (and confirmed) aspect of Terror Management Theory.[22] It is also this aspect of the theory that is most relevant here, because in an effective hegemony the worldviews of most people will be (largely) the hegemonic worldview. In an effective hegemony, worldview defense strengthens hegemonic beliefs and values, and thus strengthens consent to (and even identification with) the society one is a part of. In other words, unless hegemony is already severely weakened, violence and other reminders of death only strengthen hegemonic control.[23]

But even if hegemony is weakened, *we* cannot use violence. As explained in the chapter on hegemony, the use of force needs to be accepted: a state that uses violence against its population without hegemonic approval will lose its hegemonic control. But the same applies to counter-hegemony: if a counter-hegemonic set of values and beliefs gains strong support it will lose that support if its proponents resort to violence without the approval of the supporters. And because (rational) supporters of a set of values and beliefs centered on empathy or compassion can never approve of violence, violence is rarely an option in counter-hegemonic activism.

Rarely, but possibly not never. There may be circumstances in which the objections to instrumental violence (i.e., violence as means) do not apply. If violence is wrong because it dehumanizes the other and because it causes suffering, injury, or death, then violent actions that do not dehumanize *and* do not cause suffering, injury, or death are not wrong, or not wrong for the same reasons

22 A meta-analysis covering 164 articles on 277 experiments concluded that the Mortality Salience Hypothesis "is robust and produces moderate to large effects." See Brian L. Burke, Andy Martens, and Erik H. Faucher, "Two Decades of Terror Management Theory: A Meta-Analysis of Mortality Salience Research," *Personality and Social Psychology Review* 14.2 (2010): 155–95.

23 For the same reason, we may want to avoid using violent terminology like "war of position." It might be difficult to find good alternatives, however. Besides, while Gramsci inherited the use of militaristic terminology from other Marxist writers of the same period, as Ernesto Laclau and Chantal Mouffe have noted, "in Gramsci there is a demilitarization of war." Laclau and Mouffe, *Hegemony and Socialist Strategy: Towards a Radical Democratic Politics*, 2nd edn. (London: Verso, 2001), 70.

at least. Hence, a ban on violence is a ban on killing, injuring, and causing suffering; it is not a ban on pushing someone out of the way. And neither does it prohibit theft or arson.

Furthermore, if dehumanization and suffering are what makes violence wrong, then violence that does not dehumanize the other and that reduces (rather than increases) suffering would not be wrong. At least hypothetically, this appears to be possible.

Imagine someone who trained herself to care about everyone; someone who genuinely suffers whenever others suffer, regardless of whether she can see or hear those others, and regardless of whether she knows them. Let's call her Jane. Imagine a second person— let's call him John— who causes great suffering. As argued above, denying John compassion and killing him is not an option because it is the denial of compassion that characterizes the enemy. But what if Jane could feel compassion for John and kill him anyway, because the suffering he causes far outweighs the suffering she would cause by killing him?

An obvious reply would be that Jane isn't responsible for the suffering caused by John, while she is responsible for the suffering caused by her own actions. This reply is much too easy, however. It implies that by not doing anything you can avoid all responsibility. And it presupposes an untenable difference between acting and not-acting (or refusing to act). There is no such thing as not-acting— you are always doing something— and looking the other way doesn't let you off the hook. Besides, the question is not about responsibility, but whether Jane can use violence out of compassion and without denying anyone compassion— that is, without becoming a "monster." Hypothetically that seems possible. Whether it is actually possible, I don't know. Closest to the case of Jane killing John would be some of the stories of "compassionate killing" in ancient Buddhist literature, but those stories— as well as the notion of compassionate killing itself— are controversial.[24]

---

24 Damien Keown, "On Compassionate Killing and the Abhidhamma's 'Psychological Ethics'," *Journal of Buddhist Ethics* 23 (2016): 45–82. Whether these stories are really similar to the Jane / John case can be disputed. In many of these stories, the main reason to kill the "bad guy" is not the suffering he causes, but the damage he does to his own *karma*.

The first objection to violence is that it is monstrous, but as these last paragraphs show, this objection doesn't necessarily apply to all violence, even if exceptions may he hypothetical. Similarly, there may be exceptions to the second objection— that violence should be avoided for strategic reasons.

Violence strengthens hegemony through the increase of mortality salience, but the stronger hegemony, the smaller the relative size of this effect, and the strategic advantage of some particular act of violence may outweigh this strategic disadvantage. This too is a rather hypothetical scenario, however.[25] It requires that hegemony is almost completely unscathed (and thus cannot be strengthened much), that counter-hegemony is still almost non-existent (and thus cannot be weakened much), that there really is a strategic advantage to be gained, *and* that the monstrosity objection doesn't apply.

In other words, there may be exceptions to the general ban on violence, but these will rarely apply. Violence is rarely if ever an acceptable means in the struggle against the hegemony of psychopathy. This does not mean, however, that violence is not acceptable in *any* struggle. It may or may not be, but either claim would need an argument different from that given here.

An Uneven and Unending Struggle

Even if we abstain from violence, if the struggle against hegemony is successful, there will be violence. As argued above, it follows from Gramsci's Machiavellian theory that if in some state hegemony breaks down, the hegemones can only rely on brute force to remain in control, and the weaker hegemony, the more force is needed. And unfortunately, the hegemones have no reason to refrain from violence— in the contrary, the hegemony of psychopathy loves violence.

Hegemony will not defend itself just with violence, however, but also with manipulation, propaganda, and lies. The use of violence without consent undermines hegemony, and therefore, if other means are available, violence is not the most efficient way to suppress dissent. A much more effective tactic (which hegemony

---

25 But perhaps, there are other circumstances in which the strategic importance of some act of violence outweighs any strategic disadvantage.

is already putting to "good" use) is undermining the credibility of outspoken opponents of the hegemony of psychopathy (and / or those who threaten hegemony in other ways); by fabricating "evidence" for criminal charges, for example. We can expect much more of this. If counter-hegemonic activism gains strength, we can expect to be (falsely) accused, imprisoned, and even murdered. The hegemony of psychopathy will resist its downfall and— being psychopathic— it will stop at nothing.

If that's not enough to discourage you, there is more reason to worry. Nietzsche warned against the risk of turning into monsters when fighting monsters, but there is another warning— although not intended as such by Nietzsche himself— in the same book, *Beyond Good and Evil,* and further developed in *On the Genealogy of Morality.*[26] Nietzsche sees two threads running through the European history of moral ideas, two kinds of morality that are ever-present, sometimes even in one person. These are "master morality" and "slave morality." The first is the morality of the socio-political elite. It is a morality that values strength, control and self-control, power, and self-reliance. The second values humility, compassion, cooperation, friendliness, and so forth. While "slave morality" values and promotes empathy / compassion, master morality values a kind of self-centered hardness bordering on (cultural) psychopathy. It is master morality which Nietzsche prefers, but that is not what matters here. What does matter is Nietzsche's suggestion that this is more or less the natural morality of the socio-political elite.[27] If he is right, then perhaps the fight against the hegemony of psychopathy will never really end, because the downfall of one elite will

26 Nietzsche, *Jenseits von Gut und Böse* [*Beyond Good and Evil*]. Nietzsche, *Zur Genealogie der Moral: Eine Streitschrift* [*On the Genealogy of Morals*] (1887).

27 Some recent research seems to support this suggestion. See, for example, Paul Piff, Daniel Stancato, Stéphane Côté, Rodolfo Mendoza-Denton, and Dacher Keltner, "Higher Social Class Predicts Increased Unethical Behavior," *Proceedings of the National Academy of Sciences of the United States of America* (PNAS) 109.11 (2012): 4086–91, and Stéphane Côté, Paul Piff, and Robb Willer, "For Whom Do the Ends Justify the Means? Social Class and Utilitarian Moral Judgment," *Journal of Personality and Social Psychology* 104.3 (2013): 490–503.

(eventually) lead to the rise of another elite, which will inevitably gravitate towards (cultural) psychopathy. (See also Box 6.)

"There is no alternative," the hegemones want us to believe, and in some sense they are right. Not in the sense they intend, however— that is, not in the sense that there is no alternative to the current organization of society, to the current distribution of wealth and power, and to the currently dominant values and beliefs. Of course, there are alternatives to *that*. But there is no alternative— no *real* alternative, that is— to *fighting* the hegemony of psychopathy.

The hegemony of psychopathy is already losing strength.[28] This is why the hegemones increasingly have to resort to violence— any decrease in hegemonic control must be compensated with force. But if that use of force is insufficiently justified by hegemonic values and beliefs— and increasingly that is the case— then it only further undermines hegemony, further deteriorating hegemonic control, necessitating further compensation by force. The United States has progressed furthest on this path and seems to be destined to a slow descent into an orgy of violence, but if left unchecked, the rest of the world will follow.

The weakening of the hegemony of psychopathy is reason for concern rather than for optimism. Without a counter-hegemony to take over, destabilization can only lead to violence, and unfortunately there is little reason to believe that there is any credible counter-hegemonic force. Not even the weakening of the current hegemony can be attributed to opposing forces, but is largely the result of internal contradictions. The hegemony of psychopathy will eventually destroy itself because no society can survive the fragmentation into autonomous, egocentric parasites (i.e., psychopaths).[29] Cultural psychopathy undermines

---

28 Especially the neoliberal aspects of the current hegemony are meeting more and more resistance, but as mentioned in the previous chapter, the hegemony of psychopathy might survive the eventual collapse of the hegemony of neoliberalism, provided that it can substitute another political-economic system and produce sufficient acceptance thereof.

29 Thomas Hobbes argued that society is the product of a social contract forged between people in a "state of nature" without laws, without conventions, without morality, and so forth, in which life was "solitary, poor, nasty, brutish, and short" (*Leviathan*, 1651, XIII.9). The hegemony of psychopathy is turning Hobbesian chronology on its head, however. Rather than society

Box 6: On Nietzsche's Genealogy of Morality

According to Nietzsche, master morality and slave morality always co-existed, both in societies and in individuals, even though there are obvious conflicts between the more psychopathic master morality and the more empathic slave morality. On the social level, conflict between the two was largely avoided throughout most of history by means of a strict social separation. The elite gravitated towards master morality and the people towards slave morality, and because there was little interaction between these social classes, this was a relatively stable situation. What further promoted this stability is that people under the influence of slave morality are much easier to control. Hence, slave morality was effectively— albeit possibly not intentionally— a tool of social control.

What's different now is that the separation between the elite (or the hegemones) and the people has become somewhat more permeable, both for people (albeit more in theory than in practice) and— much more importantly— for values and beliefs. This is the reason why in the past, psychopathic master morality did not become hegemonic— the necessary infrastructure for spreading values and beliefs *throughout the whole of society* (perhaps in a loose sense of "society")[30] was still lacking. For the same reason, it is unlikely that we can return to this model. If Nietzsche is right, then— unless the elite and the rest of the people can be strictly separated, and the spreading of the elite's values and beliefs can somehow be avoided— hegemony will do "its work," and cultural psychopathy will eventually spread.[31]

cooperation, trust, and everything else that makes society possible. But by undermining society, hegemony ultimately undermines itself.

rising from a "state of nature," it disintegrates into that state. The hegemony of psychopathy slowly changes the world into a Hobbesian dystopia.

30 The concept of "society" was only invented *after* the strict separation between elite and people started to break down. If it is retrospectively applied to earlier socio-political arrangements, it may be more appropriate to speak of two parallel societies — elite society and popular / peasant society — considering that there was less interaction between those two in one "country" (noting that the use of that term is anachronistic as well) than there is between different societies now. On the history of the concept of "society," see, for example, Peter Wagner, *A History and Theory of the Social Sciences: Not All that is Solid Melts into Air* (London: Sage, 2001).

31 Except, of course, if a society invents a way to prevent this. While it is an interesting, theoretical question whether that is possible, and if so, how to do it, I do not want to engage in such Utopian (or dystopian, perhaps) speculation here.

It is important to realize, however, that what is undermined in this way is the acceptance of hegemonic control, but not the hegemonic values and beliefs. It takes a counter-hegemony to change values and beliefs. And lacking a sufficiently strong counter-hegemonic force, the deterioration of the acceptance of hegemonic control will lead to growing opposition to the socio-political status quo (and to the ruling elite in particular), but this opposition will still embody hegemonic— that is, psychopathic— values and beliefs. The most conspicuous form of such pseudo-opposition is the wave of authoritarian, so-called "populist" demagogues that have appeared mostly on the (far) right of the political spectrum.[32]

What made the Holocaust possible was a combination of uncritical, non-thinking acceptance of the ruling system and othering, the systematic dehumanization of some group of others. That uncritical acceptance— Hannah Arendt called it "the banality of evil"— is the individual's response to an effective hegemony: it is the individual's "spontaneous" (that is, uncritical, non-thinking) acceptance of and / or consent to the socio-political status quo. In other words, hegemony (as process / phenomenon) was part of what enabled the Holocaust. And importantly, the particular hegemony that enabled the Holocaust was a dehumanizing, psychopathic hegemony. Somewhat disturbingly, while according to Robert Nozick we humans have to "redeem ourselves" (see the first chapter), we have put everything in place for another holocaust instead: the hegemony of psychopathy and rampant othering.[33] Perhaps Nozick was right when he suggested that it would be "fitting" if humanity came to an end. (See also Box 7.)

But let's not give up hope yet. Either way, there will be suffering, but it is better to suffer in an attempt to reduce suffering than to stand by and watch others suffer. This, of course, is antithetical to

32 They are certainly "populist" in the sense that they make frequent use of "arguments to the people" (i.e., they abuse popular sentiments), but the term "populist" is easily abused by mainstream media to denounce anyone who threatens the status quo. (Perhaps, this implies that calling an opponent "populist" is itself populist.)

33 If the hegemony of psychopathy succeeds in breaking down all social arrangements and reduces all people to autonomous, egocentric individuals, then this will be a holocaust of all against all. That is, more or less, Hobbes' dystopian "state of nature" mentioned in note 29 above.

Box 7: The Benevolent World-Exploder

In *The Open Society and its Enemies,* Karl Popper suggested that the utilitarian principle to maximize happiness should be replaced with a principle to minimize suffering (as a political goal, at least).[34] This proposal has come to be known as "negative utilitarianism." While classical utilitarianism aims for the greatest happiness for the greatest number of people, negative utilitarianism aims for "the least amount of suffering for anybody."[35]

The best known objection to negative utilitarianism is usually called "the benevolent world-exploder" and was first put forward by Ninian Smart.[36] "Suppose that a ruler controls a weapon capable of instantly and painlessly destroying the human race." Given that this would end all human suffering, according to negative utilitarianism, that ruler would be morally obliged to use the weapon. And because "we should assuredly regard such an action as wicked," negative utilitarianism is wrong.[37]

There are many different ways in which one could respond to Smart's argument,[38] but it seems to me that its main weakness is in the last part. Smart assumes that the continuing existence of mankind is of greater moral relevance than the sum of all human suffering. Perhaps, he is right, but after the Holocaust this is no longer something that just can be assumed. There is much to be said for Nozick's assertion that "humanity has lost its claim to continue,"[39] and nothing in human history since the Holocaust has changed that. If anything, recent history only reinforces Nozick's point.

34 Karl Popper, *The Spell of Plato,* in *The Open Society and its Enemies,* Vol. 1 (London: Routledge, 1947). See especially note 6 to chapter 5 and note 2 to chapter 9.
35 Popper, *The Open Society and its Enemies,* 241n2.
36 R. Ninian Smart, "Negative Utilitarianism," *Mind* 67.268 (1958): 542–43, doi: 10.1093/mind/LXVII.268.5423.
37 Smart, "Negative Utilitarianism," 542.
38 Here's a response by analogy. Suppose some doctor proposes to the World Health Organization that it should make it its goal to eradicate measles. Humans are the only hosts of the measles virus, and thus, exterminating all humans would result in the eradication of measles. Therefore, if WHO would adopt the doctor's proposal *and* would be able to exterminate all humans, then they would (according to their newly adopted policy) be obliged to exterminate all humans.
39 Robert Nozick, "The Holocaust," in *The Examined Life: Philosophical Meditations* (New York: Simon and Schuster, 1989), 236–42; 238. Also quoted in the first chapter of this volume.

what the hegemony of psychopathy tells you— only you matter; the suffering of others is of no concern to you. Hegemony needs you to not care about others, to turn a blind eye to their suffering, to numb your natural capacity for empathy.[40] And perhaps, that's where the fight against the hegemony of psychopathy must start: with curing ourselves from the empathic numbness that hegemony relies on.

To "suffer when others do"

The ancient Chinese philosopher Mo zi, who lived in a time of nearly permanent war and disaster,[41] believed that

> if everyone under heaven [i.e., in the world] does not love each other, then the strong will surely overpower the weak, the rich will mock the poor, the gentry will play around with the menial, and cheaters will deceive the foolish. Hence, all the disasters, animosity, and hatred under heaven have arisen from the lack of mutual love.[42]

And therefore, we need universal love to solve all social and political problems, he observed.[43]

Perhaps Mo zi can be regarded as an early predecessor of the genre of Utopian empathy advocacy mentioned a few sections back.[44] If not Utopian, demanding "universal love" certainly seems to be demanding too much. The point of "curing empathic numbness" is not to learn to love everyone, let alone to love everyone equally, but— as Nozick put it— to learn to "suffer when others do." The point is to attain a genuine care for the well-being of others, especially for the reduction or elimination of others' suffering, regardless

---

40 On the "naturalness" of empathy, see, for example, Frans de Waal, *The Age of Empathy: Nature's Lessons for a Kinder Society* (New York: Three Rivers, 2009).

41 Mo zi (墨子, ca. 470–ca. 390 BCE) lived in the early Warring States Period. He traveled from one warzone to another, continuously trying to convince rulers to abstain from further bloodshed and to build defensive works to discourage others from attacking them.

42 Mo zi, "Universal Love" II (兼愛中), *Chinese Text Project,* http://ctext.org/mozi, §2. My translation.

43 See especially §4–5 of "Universal Love" I (兼愛上).

44 See "A Brief Utopian Interlude" above, in this chapter.

of whether those others are known, seen, or heard. As mentioned before, in ancient Buddhist writings something very much like this was called "*mettā*," which is usually translated as "loving-kindness." *Mettā* is empathic concern for everyone, and is to be cultivated by means of meditation (usually called "loving-kindness meditation").

Before proceeding, let me try to prevent some misunderstandings, or correct them if they have already arisen. Firstly, I'm not a Buddhist and neither am I suggesting that you become one. Secondly, and more importantly, much nonsense is spread about Buddhist meditation by the mindfulness industry. That industry promotes meditation as stress-reduction, but as pointed out by Donald Lopez and others, the goal of (at least some forms of) Buddhist meditation is stress *induction* rather than reduction.[45] Furthermore, there is no such *thing* as Buddhist meditation. Rather, there is a bewildering variety of practices and techniques that have little in common except for what they are supposed to establish: either an improvement of the ability to concentrate, or gaining specific kinds of insight. Especially meditation of the latter kind often involves study and deep thought similar to what the word "meditation" used to mean in English (and contrary to the apparent mindlessness promoted by the mindfulness industry). This variety in practices— as well as the refusal by Buddhaghosa, an influential 5th century Buddhist monk, to define the notion— suggests that "meditation" is a functional rather than a substantive category;[46] that is, "meditation" is not defined by some substantive properties that all activities called "meditation" have in common, but by those activities' function, by what meditation is intended to accomplish. If this is right, then "loving-kindness meditation" is any technique that increases *mettā* and (thus) decreases empathic numbness.

Buddhaghosa's *Visuddhimagga* is probably the best known "meditation manual." It describes a large number of meditation subjects and techniques, and argues that two of those are particularly

---

45 Donald S. Lopez, *The Scientific Buddha: His Short and Happy Life* (New Haven, CT: Yale University Press, 2012).

46 Buddhaghosa claims that meditation "is of many sorts and has various aspects" and that an attempt to define it would only "lead to distraction": *The Path of Purification (Visuddhimagga),* trans. Bhikkhu Nyanamoli (Onalaska, WA: BPS Pariyatti, 1999), III.2.

important or even essential: loving-kindness (*mettā*) and death.[47] Unfortunately, the chapter on loving-kindness is not very helpful, but the section on death as a meditation subject is.[48] In that section, Buddhaghosa writes that the meditation on death is successful only if it leads to a state of shock called "*saṃvega.*"[49] The Pāli / Sanskrit term "*saṃvega*" literally means something like (fearful) trembling, but is used in Buddhist writings to denote a morally (and religiously) motivating state of shock or agitation. Interestingly, according to Buddhaghosa, the (repeated) experience of *saṃvega* increases loving-kindness (*mettā*),[50] suggesting that the two "essential" meditation subjects (death and loving-kindness) are somehow related.

Outside the Buddhist tradition, James Baillie and I have recently written about the epistemology and psychology of *saṃvega* and / or very similar states.[51] Such "samvegic" states should be distinguished from the "normal" fear of death— that is, the slumbering background fear in the back of our minds. Samvegic shock is a state of terror caused by the sudden realization of the inevitability, finality, and utter non-negotiability of death. For some of us this state might be very familiar; others will have never experienced it. And those who have experienced it differ in their response to it: for some it was more traumatizing than for others. Baillie describes it as a state in which "rational capacities are immobilized and one is engulfed in inarticulate terror."[52]

For the lucky ones among us, this state of terror is the closest we will ever come to experiencing what it feels like to face death. But because knowing the terror of death gives one a much better

---

47 Buddhaghosa, *Visuddhimagga,* III.57–9.
48 Buddhaghosa, *Visuddhimagga,* VIII.1–41.
49 Buddhaghosa, *Visuddhimagga,* VIII.5–6.
50 Buddhaghosa, *Visuddhimagga,* XIII.35.
51 James Baillie, "The Expectation of Nothingness," *Philosophical Studies* 166.S: S185–S203. Lajos Brons, "Facing Death from a Safe Distance: *Saṃvega* and Moral Psychology," *Journal of Buddhist Ethics* 23 (2016): 83–128.
52 Baillie, "The Expectation of Nothingness," S188. Adopting a term from Thomas Nagel, Baillie calls this state "the expectation of nothingness" (Thomas Nagel, *The View from Nowhere* [Oxford: Oxford University Press, 1986]). Baillie focuses mainly on an epistemological puzzle related to this state, but also quotes some other descriptions of this state by people who experienced it and / or wrote about it.

THE WAR OF POSITION

understanding of what it is to be a victim of life-threatening violence and/or suffering, it is essential to be familiar with it. Only
if you know what it *approximately* feels like to face death can you
learn to understand (or imagine) what it is like for others to be in
a life-threatening situation. For this reason, *saṃvega* is not a state
that should be avoided, but that should be cultivated, even though
it is— obviously— far from a pleasurable experience.[53]

Buddhaghosa describes a series of meditation exercises to reach
this state of terror, the simplest of which is just repeating to yourself that you will inevitably die. What is needed to reach *saṃvega*
probably differs from person to person.[54] For someone who *firmly*
believes in some kind of life after death it may be necessary to post-
pone or bracket that belief while contemplating death, because the
point of the exercise is grasping (emotionally more than intellectually) the full meaning of the absolute inevitability, non-negotiability,
and finality of death, all of which the idea of an afterlife denies. Furthermore, the aim of the exercise is *not* to try to imagine *being* dead,
because that is impossible— almost everyone can imagine being
somewhere else or even being someone else, but it is fundamentally
impossible to imagine not existing. And for the same reason, neither does it aim for understanding *what it is like* to be dead, because
there is no such thing as *being* dead— death is not a state you can
be in; death is *not* being. The point of the exercise is to *fully* understand *that*— that death is not existing (it is not experiencing nothing, but rather not experiencing)— and its implications, *and* that
we will with absolute certainty all die. Its goal is to reach a state of
terror in which the inevitability of death— of *your* death— is not
just known and understood intellectually and emotionally, but in

53 For an analysis of the nature of *saṃvega* and its effects, also further explain-
    ing why it should be sought rather than avoided, see Brons, "Facing Death
    from a Safe Distance."
54 In addition to the exercises described here, supplementary reading on what
    it is like to be a victim of life-threatening violence may be useful, but un-
    fortunately this is a somewhat under-explored topic (within philosophy at
    least). The main exception (and recommended reading) is Susan J. Brison's
    Aftermath: Violence and the Remaking of a Self (Princeton, NJ: Princeton
    University Press, 2002), an important philosophical account of violence
    from the perspective of the victim.

which your whole body and mind shrinks away from the *full* realization that *you will die.*

Knowing the terror of death gives one a much better understanding of what it feels like to face death, but that understanding in itself is insufficient if it remains self-centered— it needs to be directed at others. To cure one's empathic numbness, it needs to be used to share in the suffering of others. This can be practiced by imagining oneself in the situation of some suffering other. The daily news provides plenty of "cases," but if you prefer, you could try to "meditate" on one of the following situations. (1) *You're a refugee on an overloaded, sinking boat in the middle of the Mediterranean, with no way to reach the shore alive.* (2) *You're a mother in a warzone, seeing your children be kicked to death by soldiers before they turn to you and put a gun against your head and pull the trigger.* (3) *You're beaten to death by an angry mob armed with stones and clubs because they believe that you did (or are) something wrong.* The aim of exercises like these is not to imagine the situations, however, nor even to imagine what the victim feels in those situation, but to *feel* what the victim feels— that is, to share in the victims' terror, probably not in all its intensity, but as close as possible. Obviously, succeeding in doing that results in an extremely distressing experience. There are several ways to relieve that stress, but crying is probably the most effective (and least damaging to your health).[55]

This is still not sufficient, however. The point of these exercises is to learn to "suffer when others do," not just to suffer with others when you choose to do so. In other words, the sharing in suffering has to become automatic. Only when empathic concern becomes a disposition, an involuntary response to others' suffering (that hits you like an unexpected kick in the guts), has one cured one's empathic numbness.

Empathic concern or compassion is our natural ability to share in the suffering of others, to suffer with them. The hegemony of psychopathy numbs and suppresses that ability— making it subversive to care for those you don't know— but that numbness is abnormal.

---

55 For a recent overview of research on the "self-soothing" and stress-reducing effects of crying, see Asmir Gračanin, Lauren M. Bylsma, and Ad J.J.M. Vingerhoets, "Is Crying a Self-Soothing Behavior?" *Frontiers in Psychology* 5.502 (2014), doi: 10.3389/fpsyg.2014.00502.

It is *not* normal to witness the suffering of others and not feel compassion and distress, but the exposure to the constant stream of violence and suffering in news and entertainment numbs the senses. A cure for this numbness must counteract the psychopathic disregard for others' suffering by restoring compassion— it must make compassion the norm (rather than the exception). Our natural ability of empathic concern can be trained or restored by placing oneself in the victims' shoes *every time* when reading, watching, or hearing news about actual human suffering, until it becomes automatic. Someone with a well-developed sense of compassion or empathic concern cannot read, see, or hear stories of suffering without feeling *some* of that suffering (but not all of it, and not all the time).

"*Saṃvega*" is sometimes translated as "sense of urgency."[56] While this may not be a literal (or even accurate) translation, it captures much of the aim of the exercises sketched above.[57] The point of those exercises is to feel others' suffering, but also to better understand the scale and extent of suffering caused by the hegemony of psychopathy. And those exercises are successful only if suffering with others becomes a permanent state, like a kind of ever-present nausea. That "nausea" gives rise to a sense of urgency indeed, as well as to abhorrence for the hegemony that causes such massive suffering.

"Compassion" literally means to suffer with others, to suffer when others do. If you're not just able to do that when it suits you or when the sufferer is close to you, but start doing it automatically and for/with anyone, then you will have cured yourself from cultural psychopathy. And then you will understand that there is no alternative indeed. We *must* fight.

---

56 This is the term Bhikkhu Nyanamoli uses in his translation of Buddhaghosa's *Visuddhimagga.*

57 And possibly also of Buddhist meditation exercises intended to reach *saṃvega.* See Brons, "Facing Death from a Safe Distance."

Epilogue

Since the 2008 global financial meltdown, growing dissent has eroded the acceptance of the socio-political status quo— and thus the strength of hegemony— but this opposition to hegemony takes two very different forms. I'll call these two different forms *Gurrian* and *Johnsonian* oppositions or rebellions here, after two theorists of political violence and dissent, Ted Gurr and Chalmers Johnson.[1] According to Gurr, the root cause of rebellion is anger directed at the established order,[2] while Johnson pointed out that political violence and dissent is often embedded in a more extensive rejection of the social foundations of the status quo and a call for social change.[3] The Gurrian/Johnsonian contrast adopted here transforms this difference in *explanation* of political violence and dissent into a difference in *kind*. That is, Gurrian opposition, which I called "pseudo-opposition" before,[4] is minimally anti-establishmentarian in the sense that it merely rejects the established representatives of hegemony, while Johnsonian opposition *also* rejects a substantial part of the hegemonic values and beliefs.

In the chapter "Hegemony" I made a distinction between direct and indirect aspects of hegemony. The former is the acceptance of

---

1   By naming these two kinds of rebellions after these two theorists, I'm not implying that the two kinds (and my descriptions of them) completely correspond to their respective theories.

2   Ted Robert Gurr, *Why Men Rebel* (Princeton, NJ: Princeton University Press, 1970).

3   Chalmers Johnson, *Revolutionary Change* (Boston, MA: Little, Brown and Company, 1966).

4   See the section "An Uneven and Unending Struggle," in Chapter 4 of this volume.

and / or consent to the socio-political status quo itself; the latter is the acceptance of and / or consent to the values and beliefs that support that status quo. Johnsonian rebellion threatens both. Gurrian rebellian, on the other hand, may *seem* to threaten the first, but only poses a threat to the socio-political status of some particular hegemones, and not to hegemony itself. That is, if successful, such a rebellion merely succeeds in replacing one representative of the hegemony of psychopathy with another. And more moderate forms of Gurrian dissent do not even undermine the established hegemones and only punish them.

The past decade has seen an increase in both kinds of opposition to hegemony, but the two kinds tend to suffer rather different fates, and for obvious reasons. Gurrian rebellion against the establishment is no real threat to hegemony and can even be used to stifle more threatening kinds of dissent. Johnsonian rebellion, on the other hand, contains the seeds of counter-hegemony, and threatens the very foundations of hegemonic control. It should not come as a surprise then that the mass media— being the main distributor of hegemonic values and beliefs and the chief manufacturer of "spontaneous" public consent— responds in very different ways to these two different kinds of dissent. Gurrian rebellion is a relatively harmless spectacle fit for the spotlight, while Johnsonian dissent— if not ignored— is marginalized, belittled, ridiculed, and undermined in every other way available. Compare, for example, the mainstream media's coverage in 2015–16 of Gurrian revolts like the Trump campaign in the US or Brexit in the UK, with more Johnsonian rebellions like the Sanders and Corbyn campaigns in those same countries. Or compare the relative media silence about (Johnsonian) anti-austerity protests and other social protest movements in many European countries with the free promotion services provided to (Gurrian) demagogues exploiting popular sentiments against minorities and refugees.

The difference in nature, treatment, fate, and background of these two kinds of opposition to hegemony reveals two serious problems. Firstly and most obviously, the observations at the end of the previous paragraph expose the make-or-break role of the mass media, which underlines the vital importance of taking control of the media and culture industry. How to do that is a good question to which I have no answer, but burning down TV stations and newspaper offices is probably not a good idea (at least from a tactical point of view). Hacktivism may be more effective, but is unlikely to be sufficient. And there are at least two further complications that need to be taken into account. The fragmentation of the media and the rise of social media have also fragmented and isolated audiences, making it increasingly difficult to reach some of them. And recent rebellions against hegemony have shown that arguments and evidence are ineffective and that sentiments rule, which suggests that hegemonic propaganda cannot be countered with reason (or at least not with reason alone).

Secondly, the examples of recent rebellions against the hegemony of psychopathy given above show that the Gurrian/Johnsonian contrast aligns with the right/left dimension of the political spectrum. All examples of Gurrian opposition are right-wing movements against the establishment, and all examples of Johnsonian opposition are left-wing movements against hegemony and (aspects of) its political-economic ideology, neoliberalism. Because only Johnsonian opposition can carry the seeds of counter-hegemony, and because the left can never win the fight against hegemony on its own, this is a very serious problem.

The root of this problem is that the right remains solidly wed to the hegemony of psychopathy, even if it occasionally opposes certain representatives or aspects thereof. The hegemonic affiliation of the right is a historical artifact, however, and not inherently necessary. On the contrary, many of the values and beliefs that are central to the hegemony of psychopathy are diametrically opposed to core values and beliefs of the communitarian and religious right.[5] The effective alliance of these parts of the political right with cultural psychopathy and neoliberalism makes their ideologies incoherent, but only when communitarian and religious movements *themselves* realize that hegemony is their enemy can they become allies in the fight against hegemony.

Unfortunately, incoherence is not the main problem on the right of the political spectrum— that dubious honor goes to the rise of neo-fascism. Fascism is a family of political ideologies that combine most or all of the following *-isms*: authoritarianism, nationalism/patriotism, anti-liberalism, racism/supremacism (and rabid

---

5   But not of the libertarian right, which celebrates cultural psychopathy.

othering in general), anti-feminism, anti-intellectualism/anti-scientism, and reactionary utopianism (that is, the idealization of some time in the past when the country was still "great" and that it needs to return to). What distinguishes neo-fascism from fascism is that, while 20th-century fascist ideologies had economic programs that awarded a key role to the state, neo-fascism tends to align itself economically with neoliberalism (although not necessarily consistently). Because of this, and because neo-fascism is— to some extent— cultural psychopathy on steroids, it is no serious threat to hegemony. Consequently, neo-fascist revolts against the establishment are Gurrian, and in an increasing number of countries it is the political establishment itself that turns to neo-fascism as a means to retain hegemonic control.

However, while neo-fascism is not a threat to hegemony, and may even be a useful tool to manufacture popular acceptance of the oppression of dissent, it is— rather obviously— a very serious threat to anyone who does not or cannot conform, and this raises a question. I wrote above that— except in rather hypothetical circumstances— violence is not an acceptable tool in the fight against hegemony, but would violence be acceptable in the fight against neo-fascism?

I don't know. The question of violence— whether and when it is legitimate and/or strategically advantageous in political struggle— is by far the most difficult question addressed in this essay, and my answer to this question in the last chapter is only provisional. Because violence always causes suffering, it is always wrong,[6] but *perhaps* it can be argued that when the choice is between less and much more suffering, then the choice should be for the first. Such a line of argument could be used to defend the use of violence to avoid greater suffering, but would not address the "monstrosity objection" to the use of violence explained above.[7] Maybe that objection becomes void when the stakes are high enough, but this suggestion risks answering the question of violence with a calculus of suffering that abstracts away the individual sufferer, thus

---

6 Assuming that (causing) suffering is always wrong, of course. For an argument for the wrongness of suffering, see Derek Parfit, *On What Matters* (New York: Oxford University Press, 2011), 565–69.
7 See the section "The Monstrosity of Violence," in chapter 4 of this volume.

effectively taking compassion out of the equation. And therefore, that cannot be the right answer. But rejecting all violence just to avoid becoming a "monster" when some particular act of violence would avoid (or reduce) massive suffering certainly cannot be the right answer either. (Surely, timidly looking away and refusing to act is just as monstrous.) And there *will* be massive suffering, and therefore, answering the question of violence is not just a theoretical problem.

There already is massive suffering— in war zones and much of the Third World, for example— but there will be more. Much more. There is a serious risk that the rise of neo-fascism leads to a much larger war than any the world has seen in the last half century, but there is an even greater source of future suffering that hasn't been mentioned in this essay or even hinted at yet: climate change. Sea level rise, desertification, mega-storms, and various other effects of climate change will lead to disasters, famines, and refugee flows well beyond anything mankind has ever experienced. By the end of the current century hundreds of millions of people will be displaced or killed by the effects of climate change. And the economic and political fall-out will affect many more.[8]

It is doubtful that this can be avoided. Global temperatures and ocean levels are already rising, storms and other extreme weather are already getting worse, desertification is already spreading, and probably we have already passed some tipping points beyond which various feedback effects started taking effect. In other words, most likely it is already too late, but even if it isn't, the political will to deal with climate change has always been a few decades behind what is actually necessary, and there is no reason to expect that this will suddenly change.[9]

8   See, for example, Gwynne Dyer, *Climate Wars: The Fight for Survival as the World Overheats* (Oxford, UK: Oneworld, 2010).

9   See Dyer, *Climate Wars*. The most recent intergovernmental agreement on climate change is the Paris Agreement (COP21). Although this agreement is likely to go into "force," that "force" amounts to nothing as it lacks concrete goals or targets and cannot be enforced. The Paris Agreement is much too little and much too late to stop catastrophic climate change. On this point, see Clive Hamilton, *Requiem for a Species: Why We Resist the Truth about Climate Change* (New York: Earthscan, 2010). See also J. Rogelj et al., "Paris Agreement Climate Proposals Need a Boost to Keep Warming Well Below

One may wonder: What is the point of fighting hegemony if we cannot stop massive suffering anyway? But we can alleviate it. It will make an enormous difference if a future society responds with compassion to disaster and refugee flows, rather than with cultural psychopathy. We should aim to avoid the secondary disasters caused by indifference and abandonment of the victims, but we can only do so by destroying cultural psychopathy and the systems that promote it. If we cannot do that, if we cannot build some better, more compassionate future on the ruins of the one we (once) thought we had, if we can only respond to the suffering we have caused with causing even more suffering, then we are a more loathsome species than anything that has ever lived on this planet, and we'd better go extinct.

The hegemony of psychopathy has destroyed everything, including the future. Now we must destroy that hegemony.

Or die trying.

2°C," *Nature* 534.7609 (2016): 631–39, doi: 10.1038/nature18307.

References

Abraham, Eyal, Talma Hendler, Irit Shapira-Lichter, Yaniv Kanat-Maymon, Orna Zagoory-Sharon, and Ruth Feldman. "Father's Brain is Sensitive to Childcare Experiences." *Proceedings of the National Academy of Sciences of the United States of America* (PNAS) 111.27 (2014): 9792–97. Doi: 10.1073/pnas.1402569111.

Ali, Tariq. *The Extreme Centre: A Warning.* London: Verso, 2015.

Arendt, Hannah. *Eichmann in Jerusalem: A Report on the Banality of Evil.* New York: Viking, 1963.

———. "On Violence." In *Crises of the Republic: Lying in Politics; Civil Disobedience; On Violence; Thoughts on Politics and Revolution,* 101–98. New York: Harcourt Brace Jovanovich, 1972.

Audi, Robert. "On the Meaning and Justification of Violence." In *Violence: Award Winning Essays in the Council for Philosophical Studies Competition,* ed. Jerome A. Shaffer, 45–99. New York: McKay, 1971.

Bailin, Sharon, and Harvey Siegel. "Critical Thinking." In *The Blackwell Guide to the Philosophy of Education,* edited by Nigel Blake, Paul Smeyers, Richard Smith, and Paul Standish, 181–193. Malden, MA: Blackwell, 2003.

Baillie, James. "The Expectation of Nothingness." *Philosophical Studies* 166.S (2013): S185–S203.

Baron-Cohen, Simon. *The Science of Evil: On Empathy and the Origins of Cruelty.* New York: Basic Books, 2011.

Bakan, Joel. *The Corporation: The Pathological Pursuit of Profit and Power.* New York: Free Press, 2004.

Batson, C. Daniel. *The Altruism Question: Toward a Social-Psychological Answer.* Hillsdale, NJ: Erlbaum, 1991.

———. "The Things Called Empathy: Eight Related but Distinct Phenomena." In *The Social Neuroscience of Empathy,* eds. Jean Decety and William John Ickes, 3–15. Cambridge, MA: MIT Press, 2009.

———. *Altruism in Humans.* New York: Oxford University Press, 2011.

———. *What's Wrong with Morality? A Social-Psychological Perspective.* Oxford, UK: Oxford University Press, 2016.

———, Jay Coke, M.L. Jasnoski, and Michael Hanson. "Buying Kindness: Effect of an Extrinsic Incentive for Helping on Perceived Altruism." *Personality and Social Psychology Bulletin* 4.1 (1978): 86–91.

Bloom, Paul. *Against Empathy: The Case for Rational Compassion.* London: Bodley Head, 2016.

Boothman, Derek. "The Sources for Gramsci's Concept of Hegemony." *Rethinking Marxism* 20.2 (2008): 201–15. Doi: 10.1080/08935690801916942.

Bowles, Samuel. "Policies Designed for Self-Interested Citizens May Undermine 'The Moral Sentiments': Evidence from Economic Experiments." *Science* 320.5883 (2008): 1605–9.

Braver, Lee. *A Thing of This World: A History of Continental Anti-Realism.* Evanston, IL: Northwestern University Press, 2007.

Brison, Susan J. *Aftermath: Violence and the Remaking of a Self.* Princeton, NJ: Princeton University Press, 2002.

Brons, Lajos. "Dharmakīrti, Davidson, and Knowing Reality." *Comparative Philosophy* 3.1 (2012): 30–57.

———. "Meaning and Reality: A Cross-Traditional Encounter." In *Constructive Engagement of Analytic and Continental Approaches in Philosophy,* eds. Bo Mou and Richard Tieszen, 199–200. Leiden: Brill, 2013.

———. "Othering, an Analysis." *Transcience: A Journal of Global Studies* 6.1 (2015): 69–90.

———. "Anarchism as Metaphilosophy." *The Science of Mind* 53 (2015): 139–58.

———. "Facing Death from a Safe Distance: *Saṃvega* and Moral Psychology." *Journal of Buddhist Ethics* 23 (2016): 83–128.

Browning, Christopher R. *Ordinary Men: Reserve Police Battalion 101 and the Final Solution in Poland.* New York: HarperCollins, 1998.

Bryant, Levi, Nick Srnicek, and Graham Harman. "Towards a Speculative Philosophy." In *The Speculative Turn: Continental Materialism and Realism,* eds. Levi Bryant, Nick Srnicek, and Graham Harman, 1–18. Melbourne, Australia: re.press, 2011.

Buddhaghosa. *The Path of Purification (Visuddhimagga),* trans. Bhikkhu Nyanamoli. Onalaska, WA: BPS Pariyatti, 1999.

Burke, Brian L., Andy Martens, and Erik H. Faucher. "Two Decades of Terror Management Theory: A Meta-Analysis of Mortality Salience Research." *Personality and Social Psychology Review* 14.2 (2010): 155–95.

Chang, Ha-Joon. *Kicking away the Ladder.* London: Anthem, 2002.

———. *Bad Samaritans: Rich Nations, Poor Policies, and the Threat to the Developing World.* London: Random House Business, 2007.

———. *23 Things They Don't Tell You about Capitalism.* London: Penguin, 2010.

Clark, Lee Anna. "Assessment and Diagnosis of Personality Disorder: Perennial Issues and an Emerging Reconceptualization." *Annual Review of Psychology* 58.1 (2007): 227–57.

Cleckley, Hervey M. *The Mask of Sanity: An Attempt to Clarify Some Issues about the So-called Psychopathic Personality.* 1st and 5th edns. St. Louis, MO: Mosby, 1941 and 1976.

Coady, C.A.J. "The Idea of Violence." *Journal of Applied Philosophy* 3.1 (1986): 3–19. Doi: 10.1111/j.1468-5930.1986.tb00045.x.

Cooke, David J., Christine Michie, Stephen D. Hart, and Daniel A. Clark. "Reconstructing Psychopathy: Clarifying the Significance of Antisocial and Socially Deviant Behavior in the Diagnosis of Psychopathic Personality Disorder." *Journal of Personality Disorders* 18.4 (2004): 337–57.

Côté, Stéphane, Paul Piff, and Robb Willer. "For Whom Do the Ends Justify the Means? Social Class and Utilitarian Moral Judgment." *Journal of Personality and Social Psychology* 104.3 (2013): 490–503.

Davies, William. *The Happiness Industry: How the Government and Big Business Sold us Well-Being.* London: Verso, 2015.

De Beauvoir, Simone. *Le Deuxième Sexe.* Paris: Gallimard, 1949. Reprint, 1976.

De Waal, Frans. *The Age of Empathy: Nature's Lessons for a Kinder Society.* New York: Three Rivers, 2009.

Derrida, Jacques. *De la Grammatologie.* Paris: Les Éditions de Minuit, 1967.

Drakulić, Slavenka. *The Balkan Express: Fragments from the Other Side of the War.* New York: Norton, 1993.

Dubois, David, Derek Rucker, and Adam Galinsky. "Social Class, Power, and Selfishness: When and Why Upper and Lower Class Individuals Behave Unethically." *Journal of Personality and Social Psychology* 108.3 (2015): 436–49.

Dyer, Gwynne. *Climate Wars: The Fight for Survival as the World Overheats.* Oxford, UK: Oneworld, 2010.

Evans, Brad and Henry A. Giroux. *Disposable Futures: The Seduction of Violence in the Age of Spectacle.* San Francisco, CA: City Lights, 2015.

Ferraro, Fabrizio, Jeffrey Pfeffer, and Robert I. Sutton. "Economics Language and Assumptions: How Theories can Become Self-Fulfilling." *Academy of Management Review* 30.1 (2005): 8–24.

Fisher, Mark. *Capitalist Realism: Is There no Alternative?* Winchester, VA: Zero Books, 2009.

Fontana, Benedetto. "Hegemony and Power in Gramsci." In *Hegemony: Studies in Consensus and Coercion,* eds. Richard Howson and Kylie Smith, 80–106. New York: Routledge, 2008.

Foucault, Michel. *The Birth of Biopolitics: Lectures at the College de France, 1978-1979,* ed. Michael Senellart, trans. Graham Burchell. New York: Palgrave Macmillan, 2008.

Galeo, Sandra, Melissa Tracy, Katherine J. Hogatt, Charles DiMaggio, and Adam Karpati. "Estimated Deaths Attributable to Social Factors in the United States." *American Journal of Public Health* 101.8 (2011): 1456–65.

Gallie, W.B. "Essentially contested concepts." *Proceedings of the Aristotelian Society* 56 (1956): 167–98.

Galtung, Johan. "Violence, Peace, and Peace Research." *Journal of Peace Research* 6.3 (1969): 167–91.

Garver, Newton. "What Violence Is." In *Philosophy for a New Generation,* eds. A.K. Bierman and James A. Gould, 2nd edn., 256–66. New York: Macmillan, 1973. Doi: 10.2307/2105905.

Geras, Norman. *The Contract of Mutual Indifference: Political Philosophy After the Holocaust.* London: Verso, 1998.

Giacalone, Robert, and Mark D. Promisto. "Broken When Entering: The Stigmatization of Goodness and Business Ethics Education." *Academy of Management Learning & Education* 12.1 (2012): 81–101.

Gilligan, Carroll. *In a Different Voice: Psychological Theory and Women's Development.* Cambridge, MA: Harvard University Press, 1982.

Gračanin, Asmir, Lauren M. Bylsma, and Ad J.J.M. Vingerhoets. "Is Crying a Self-Soothing Behavior?" *Frontiers in Psychology* 5.502 (2014). Doi: 10.3389/ fpsyg.2014.00502.

Gramsci, Antonio. *Selections from the Prison Notebooks.* New York: International Publishers, 1971.

Greenberg, Jeff, and J. Arndt. "Terror Management Theory." In *Handbook of Theories of Social Psychology,* 2 vols., eds. Paul A.M. Van Lange, Arie W. Kruglanski, and E. Tony Higgins, 1:398–415. London: Sage, 2012.

Gurr, Ted Robert. *Why Men Rebel.* Princeton, NJ: Princeton University Press, 1970.

Hamilton, Clive. *Requiem for a Species: Why We Resist the Truth about Climate Change.* New York: Earthscan, 2010.

Hamilton, David. "The Ceremonial Aspect of Corporate Organization." *American Journal of Economics and Sociology* 16.1 (1956): 11–24.

———. "The Entrepreneur as Cultural Hero." *The Southwestern Social Science Quarterly* 38.3 (1957): 248–56.

Hare, Robert D. "A Research Scale for the Assessment of Psychopathy in Criminal Populations." *Personality and Individual Differences* 1.2 (1980): 111–19.

———. *The Hare Psychopathy Checklist—Revised.* 1st and 2nd edns. Toronto, Canada: Multi-Health Systems, 1991 and 2003.

———, and Craig S. Neumann. "Psychopathy as a Clinical and Empirical Construct." *Annual Review of Clinical Psychology* 4 (2008): 217–46.

Häring, Norbert, and Niall Douglas. *Economists and the Powerful: Convenient Theories, Distorted Facts, Ample Rewards*. London: Anthem, 2012.

Harvey, David. *A Brief History of Neoliberalism*. Oxford, UK: Oxford University Press, 2007.

Heider, Fritz. *The Psychology of Interpersonal Relations*. New York: Wiley, 1958.

Hill, Robert, and Gregory Yousey. "Adaptive and Maladaptive Narcissism among University Faculty, Clergy, Politicians, and Librarians." *Current Psychology* 17.2 (1998): 163–69.

Hobbes, Thomas. *Leviathan*. 1651.

Horkheimer, Max, and Theodor W. Adorno. *Dialektik der Aufklärung*. Amsterdam: Querido, 1947.

Hudson, Michael. "Technical Progress and Obsolescence of Capital and Skills: Theoretical Foundations of Nineteenth-Century US Industrial and Trade Policy." In *Globalization, Economic Development and Inequality: An Alternative Perspective,* ed. Erik Reinert, 100–111. Cheltenham, UK: Edward Elgar, 2004.

Hühn, Mathias Philip. "You Reap What You Sow: How MBA Programs Undermine Ethics." *Journal of Business Ethics* 121 (2014): 527–41.

Hyde, Janet S. "The Gender Similarities Hypothesis." *American Psychologist* 60.6 (2005): 571–92.

Jaffee, Sara, and Janet S. Hyde. "Gender Differences in Moral Orientation: A Meta-Analysis." *Psychological Bulletin* 126 (2000): 703–26.

Jameson, Fredric. *Postmodernism; or, the Cultural Logic of Late Capitalism*. Durham, NC: Duke University Press, 1991.

———. "Future City." *New Left Review* 21 (2003): 65–79.

Johnson, Alan. "Slavoj Žižek's Theory of Revolution: A Critique." In *The Legacy of Marxism: Contemporary Challenges, Conflicts, and Developments,* ed. Matthew Johnson, 37–55. London: Continuum, 2012.

Johnson, Chalmers. *Revolutionary Change*. Boston, MA: Little, Brown, 1966.

Jonason, Peter K., Gregory D. Webster, David P. Schmitt, Norman P. Li, and Laura Crysel. "The Antihero in Popular Culture: Life History Theory and the Dark Triad Personality Traits." *Review of General Psychology* 16.2 (2012): 192–99.

Kaplan, Laura Duhan. "Teaching Intellectual Autonomy: The Failure of the Critical Thinking Movement." In *Re-Thinking Reason: New Perspectives on Critical Thinking,* ed. Kerry S. Walters, 205–20. Albany: State University of New York Press, 1994.

Katzner, Donald W. "A Neoclassical Curmudgeon Looks at Heterodox Criticisms of Microeconomics." *World Economic Review* 4 (2015): 63–75.

Keown, Damien. "On Compassionate Killing and the Abhidhamma's 'Psychological Ethics'." *Journal of Buddhist Ethics* 23 (2016): 45–82.

Kim, Pilyoung, Paola Rigo, Linda C. Mayes, Ruth Feldman, James F. Leckman, and James E. Swain. "Neural Plasticity in Fathers of Human Infants." *Social Neuroscience* 9.5 (2014): 522–35.

Kraus, Michael, Paul Piff, Rodolfo Mendoza-Denton, Michelle Rheinschmidt, and Dacher Keltner. "Social Class, Solipsism, and Contextualism: How the Rich are Different from the Poor." *Psychological Review* 119.3 (2012): 546–72.

Kripke, Saul. *Naming and Necessity.* Oxford, UK: Blackwell, 1972. Reprint, 1980.

Laclau, Ernesto, and Chantal Mouffe. *Hegemony and Socialist Strategy: Towards a Radical Democratic Politics.* 2nd edn. London: Verso, 2001.

Landau, Iddo. "Good Women and Bad Men: A Bias in Feminist Research." *Journal of Social Philosophy* 28.1 (1997): 141–50. Doi: 10.1111/j.1467-9833.1997.tb00369.x.

Latour, Bruno. "Why Has Critique Run out of Steam? From Matters of Fact to Matters of Concern." *Critical Inquiry* 30.2 (2004): 225–48.

Lopez, Donald S. *The Scientific Buddha: His Short and Happy Life.* New Haven, CT: Yale University Press, 2012.

Lukes, Steven. *Power: A Radical View.* Basingstoke, UK: Palgrave Macmillan, 1974.

Marples, Roger, ed. *The Aims of Education.* London: Routledge, 1999.

Marx, Karl. *Thesen über Feuerbach.* 1845. In Karl Marx and Friedrich Engels, *Werke,* Vol. 3, 5–7. Berlin: Dietz, 1969.

Miller, Dale T. "The Norm of Self-Interest." *American Psychologist* 54.12 (1999): 1053–60.

THE HEGEMONY OF PSYCHOPATHY

Mitchell, Timothy. "Fixing the Economy." *Cultural Studies* 12.1 (1998): 82–101.

Mo zi (墨子). *Mo zi (墨子). Chinese Text Project.* http://ctext.org/mozi.

Nagel, Thomas. *The View from Nowhere.* Oxford, UK: Oxford University Press, 1986.

Negri, Antonio. *The Politics of Subversion: A Manifesto for the Twenty-First Century.* Cambridge, UK: Polity Press, 1989.

Nietzsche, Friedrich. *Jenseits von Gut und Böse: Vorspiel einer Philosophie der Zukunft* [*Beyond Good and Evil*]. 1886.

———. *Zur Genealogie der Moral: Eine Streitschrift* [*On the Genealogy of Morals*]. 1887.

Noddings, Nel. *Caring: A Feminine Approach to Ethics and Moral Education.* Berkeley, CA: University of California Press, 1984.

Norberg, Johan. *Progress: Ten Reasons to Look Forward to the Future.* Oxford, UK: Oneworld, 2016.

Nozick, Robert. "The Holocaust." In *The Examined Life: Philosophical Meditations,* 236–42. New York: Simon and Schuster, 1989.

Nussbaum, Martha. *Not for Profit: Why Democracy Needs the Humanities.* Princeton, NJ: Princeton University Press, 2010.

———. *Anger and Forgiveness: Resentment, Generosity, Justice.* New York: Oxford University Press, 2016.

Olson, Gary. *Empathy Imperiled: Capitalism, Culture, and the Brain.* New York: Springer, 2013.

Parfit, Derek. *On What Matters.* Vol. 1. New York: Oxford University Press, 2011.

Paul, Richard. "The State of Critical Thinking Today." *New Directions for Community Colleges* 130 (2005): 27–38. Doi: 10.1002/cc.193.

Piff, Paul. "Wealth and the Inflated Self: Class, Entitlement, and Narcissism." *Personality and Social Psychology Bulletin* 40.1 (2014): 34–43.

———, Daniel Stancato, Stéphane Côté, Rodolfo Mendoza-Denton, and Dacher Keltner. "Higher Social Class Predicts Increased Unethical Behavior." *Proceedings of the National Academy of Sciences of the United States of America* (PNAS) 109.11 (2012): 4086–91.

110

Pinker, Steven. *The Better Angels of Our Nature: Why Violence Has Declined.* New York: Viking, 2011.

Plato. *Apology.*

Popovic, Srdja, and Matthew Miller. *Blueprint for Revolution: How to Use Rice Pudding, Lego Men, and Other Non-Violent Techniques to Galvanize Communities, Overthrow Dictators, or Simply Change the World.* Brunswick, Australia: Scribe, 2015.

Popper, Karl. *The Spell of Plato. The Open Society and its Enemies.* Vol. 1. London: Routledge, 1947.

Quiggin, John. *Zombie Economics: How Dead Ideas Still Walk Among Us.* Princeton, NJ: Princeton University Press, 2010.

Reinert, Erik S. *How Rich Countries Got Rich . . . and Why Poor Countries Stay Poor.* London: Constable, 2007.

———. "Neo-classical Economics: A Trail of Economic Destruction Since the 1970s." *Real World Economics Review* 60 (2012): 2–17.

———, and Arno M. Daastøl. "The Other Canon: The History of Renaissance Economics." In *Globalization, Economic Development and Inequality: An Alternative Perspective,* ed. Erik S. Reinert, 21–70. Cheltenham, UK: Edward Elgar, 2004.

Reisch, George. *How the Cold War Transformed the Philosophy of Science.* Cambridge, UK: Cambridge University Press, 2005.

Rogelj, Joeri, Michael den Elzen, Niklas Höhne, Taryn Fransen, Hanna Fekete, Harald Winkler, Roberto Schaeffer, Fu Sha, Keywan Riahl, and Malte Meinshausen. "Paris Agreement climate proposals need a boost to keep warming well below 2°C." *Nature* 534 (2016): 631–39.

Ruddick, Sara. *Maternal Thinking: Towards a Politics of Peace.* Boston, MA: Beacon, 1989.

Said, Edward. *Orientalism.* New York: Pantheon Books, 1978.

Saltman, Kenneth. "Learning to be a Psychopath: The Pedagogy of the Corporation." In *Critical Pedagogy and Global Literature: Worldly Teaching,* eds. Masood Raja, Hillary Stringer, and Zach Vandezande, 47–62. New York: Palgrave MacMillan, 2013.

Schumpeter, Joseph A. Preface. In Frederik Zeuthen, *Problems of Monopoly and Economic Warfare,* vii–xiii. London: Routledge, 1930.

Schwitzgebel, Eric. "A Theory of Jerks." *Aeon Magazine,* June 4, 2014. http://aeon.co/magazine/philosophy/if-youre-surrounded-by-idiots-guess-whos-the-jerk/.

Searle, John. *The Construction of Social Reality.* New York: The Free Press, 1995.

Sherman, David K., and Geoffrey L. Cohen. "The Psychology of Self-Defense: Self-Affirmation Theory." *Advances in Experimental Social Psychology* 38 (2006): 183–242.

Siegel, H. "Educating Reason: Critical Thinking, Informal Logic, and the Philosophy of Education— Part Two: Philosophical Questions Underlying Education for Critical Thinking." *Informal Logic* 7.2&3 (1985): 69–81. Doi: 10.22329/il.v7i2.2706.

Singer, Peter. "Famine, Affluence, and Morality." *Philosophy and Public Affairs* 1.3 (1972): 229–43.

Smart, R. Ninian. "Negative Utilitarianism." *Mind* 67.268 (1958): 542–43. Doi: 10.1093/mind/LXVII.268.5423.

Solomon, Sheldon, Jeff Greenberg, and Thomas A. Pyszczynski. *The Worm at the Core: On the Role of Death in Life.* New York: Random House, 2015.

Stellar, Jennifer, Vida Manzo, Michael Kraus, and Dacher Keltner. "Class and Compassion: Socioeconomic Factors Predict Responses to Suffering." *Emotion* 12.3 (2012): 449–59.

Storey, Anne E., and Toni E. Ziegler. "Primate Paternal Care: Interactions between Biology and Social Experience." *Hormones and Behavior* 77 (2016): 260–71.

Storm, Servaas, and C.W.M. Naastepad. *Macroeconomics beyond the NAIRU.* Cambridge, MA: Harvard University Press, 2012.

———. "Europe's Hunger Games: Income Distribution, Cost Competitiveness and Crisis." *Cambridge Journal of Economics* 39.3 (2015): 959–86.

Streeck, Wolfgang. "How Will Capitalism End?" *New Left Review* 87 (2014): 35–64.

Tajfel, Henri, and John C. Turner. "An Integrative Theory of Intergroup Conflict." In *The Social Psychology of Intergroup Relations,* eds. William G. Austin and Stephen Worchel, 33–47. Monterey, CA: Brooks-Cole, 1979.

Twenge, Jean M., and W. Keith Campbell. *The Narcissism Epidemic: Living in the Age of Entitlement.* New York: Atria, 2009.

Varoufakis, Yanis. *Economic Indeterminacy: A Personal Encounter with the Economists' Peculiar Nemesis.* London: Routledge, 2014.

Veblen, Thorstein. "Why Is Economics Not an Evolutionary Science?" *The Quarterly Journal of Economics* 12.4 (1898): 373–97.

Wagner, Peter. *A History and Theory of the Social Sciences: Not All that is Solid Melts into Air.* London: Sage, 2001.

Wang, Long, Deepak Malhotra, and J. Keith Murninghan. "Economics Education and Greed." *Management Learning & Education* 10.4 (2011): 643–60.

Weeks, John F. *Economics of the 1%: How Mainstream Economics Serves the Rich, Obscures Reality and Distorts Policy.* London: Anthem, 2014.

Wheeler, Samuel. *Neo-Davidsonian Metaphysics: From the True to the Good.* New York: Routledge, 2014.

"The local mechanisms of mind . . . are not all in the head.

Cognition leaks out into body and world."

— Andy Clark, *Supersizing the Mind*

brainstorm books

Current developments in psychoanalysis, psychology, philosophy, and cognitive and neuroscience confirm the profound importance of expression and interpretation in forming the mind's re-workings of its intersubjective, historical and planetary environments. Brainstorm Books seeks to publish cross-disciplinary work on the becomings of the extended and enactivist mind, especially as afforded by semiotic experience. Attending to the centrality of expression and impression to living process and to the ecologically-embedded situatedness of mind is at the heart of our enterprise. We seek to cultivate and curate writing that attends to the ways in which art and aesthetics are bound to, and enhance, our bodily, affective, cognitive, developmental, intersubjective, and transpersonal practices.

Brainstorm Books is an imprint of the "Literature and the Mind" group at the University of California, Santa Barbara, a research and teaching concentration hosted within the Department of English and supported by affiliated faculty in Comparative Literature, Religious Studies, History, the Life Sciences, Psychology, Cognitive Science, and the Arts.

http://mind.english.ucsb.edu/brainstorm-books